WORLD HISTORY

Classical Civilization:
Greece

WORLD
HISTORY

WORLD HISTORY: CLASSICAL CIVILIZATION: GREECE
Copyright © 2012 by Morgan Reynolds Publishing

Library of Congress Cataloging-in-Publication Data

Nardo, Don, 1947-
Classical civilization : Greece / by Don Nardo.
    p. cm. -- (World history)
Includes bibliographical references and index.
ISBN 978-1-59935-173-5 (alk. paper) -- 978-1-59935-302-9 (e-book)
1. Greece--Civilization--To 146 B.C.--Juvenile literature. 2.
Greece--History--To 146 B.C.--Juvenile literature. I. Title.
DF215.N36 2012
938--dc22

                          2011000235

PRINTED IN THE UNITED STATES OF AMERICA
First Edition

Book cover and interior designed by:
Ed Morgan, navyblue design studio
Greensboro, NC

WORLD HISTORY

Classical Civilization: Greece

Don Nardo

Greensboro, North Carolina

Table of Contents

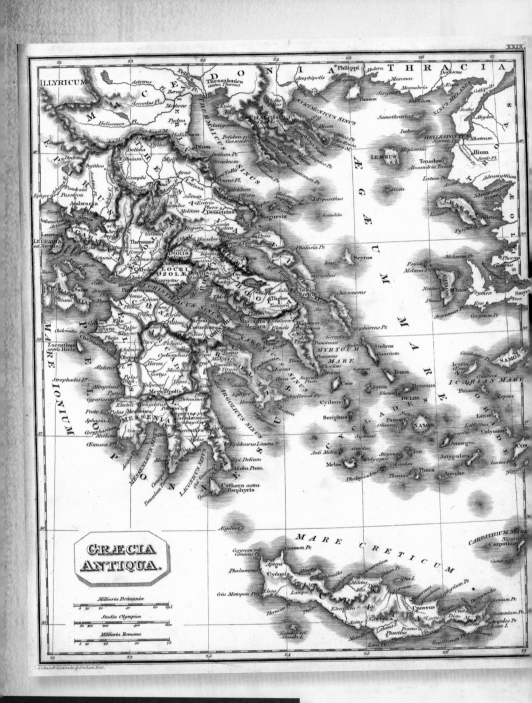

A vintage map of Ancient Greece

Chapter One:
A Brief History of Ancient Greece

Archaeologists and historians still do not know for sure when humans first arrived in what is now Greece. Some evidence indicates that primitive hunter-gatherers were living there at least 50,000 years ago. As that descriptive term suggests, they sustained themselves by hunting animals and gathering berries, roots, and other wild plant products. Like people living in other parts of the world at that time, the weapons and tools they used were made of stone.

Major advances came when Greece's inhabitants began exploiting metal weapons, tools, and other objects. They were using copper by about 6000 BCE (8,000 years ago) and bronze, an alloy, or mixture, of copper and tin, by roughly 3,000 BCE. (Modern scholars call the period in which bronze was the main metal in use the Bronze Age. It lasted from about 3000 to 1100 BCE.) Because bronze spearheads and knives are harder and keep their edges longer than stone or copper ones, hunting, slaughtering animals, and other activities became more efficient. Also, bronze was seen as more valuable than copper. And silver and gold, which people were able to extract in small amounts by 2500 BCE, were even more precious. As scholar Sarah B. Pomeroy explains, ownership of metals led to important social and economic developments:

> High-ranked individuals and families, those with greater surpluses of wealth, [had] the most access to bronze and [silver and gold] products. Possession of these and other prestige items set them further apart from the mass of the population. . . . Early Bronze Age Greece was edging its way into the wider economy and culture of the Mediterranean world. And as the economy expanded and the settlements grew larger, so did the wealth, power, and authority of their leaders, now established as hereditary chiefs who ruled for life and were accorded exceptional honors and privileges.

In this way, nobles, or aristocrats, arose in settlements across the Greek lands. (The term aristocrat comes from the Greek word *aristoi*, meaning "best people.")

Two Early Cultural Spheres

The lands in which early Greek civilization grew were divided into two general geographic and cultural spheres in the late Bronze Age (ca. 1600-1150 BCE). The first and most influential was centered on the large Aegean island of Crete and smaller surrounding islands. There, a highly civilized people, dubbed the Minoans by modern scholars, erected several large, splendid palace-centers. Historian Charles Freeman writes:

These were sophisticated buildings, adorned with large courtyards and colorful frescoes [paintings done on wet plaster]. They acted as centers for the gathering and recording of local agricultural produce that was then traded overseas for stone and metals. Minoan traders were found throughout the southern Aegean [and] evidence of communities of Minoan craftsmen has been found in northern Egypt [and] modern Israel.

Meanwhile, in the other major sphere, the Greek mainland, a people now called the Mycenaeans (after their chief fortress-town of Mycenae, in the mainland's southeastern sector), held sway. They, too, built large palaces, though smaller and less complex and sophisticated than those in Crete. For a few centuries, the Mycenaeans appear to have been culturally influenced by the Minoans. The latter may also have politically dominated the mainlanders, though scholars still debate this.

Whatever the relationship between the two peoples may have been, in about 1400 BCE Mycenaean warlords invaded Crete. They took over the palace-centers, as well as the eastern Mediterranean trade routes and markets long exploited by the Minoans. In the two centuries that followed, the Mycenaeans flourished. Evidence suggests that they regularly visited Egypt and often raided the coasts of Anatolia (what is now Turkey).

One of those raids, likely occurring between 1250 and 1200 BCE, was on the Anatolian city of Troy. It appears that the memory of that event, passed on orally over later generations, was the source of the famous legend of the Trojan War. Said oral tradition culminated in the eighth-century BCE. Many historians think that a Greek poet of that time, Homer, produced the most elaborate version of the story and dictated it to a scribe. The result was two long, magnificent epic poems—the *Iliad* and *Odyssey*, which exerted major literary and social influences on the Greeks in later centuries.

The Dark Age and Its Aftermath

The Trojan War, if it was indeed a real event, was probably one of the last successful Mycenaean military ventures. Not long after 1200 BCE the Aegean region, along with large portions of the western Middle East, plunged into an extended period of political, social, and military turmoil. In the span of a generation or two, a majority of the Mycenaeans' palaces were attacked and burned and their civilization rapidly declined and disintegrated. The exact reasons for this widespread upheaval are still not well understood. Theories advanced to explain it include economic collapse, civil strife, and incursions of warlike peoples from the regions northwest of Greece. Whatever the cause or causes, large-scale political organization, writing, and other features of civilized life for the most part disappeared. And Greece entered an era that historians refer to as its Dark Age.

During the Dark Age, which lasted from about 1100 to 800 BCE, Greece's population decreased significantly and poverty became widespread. Also, "the palace-centers were in ruins or uninhabited," Pomeroy remarks:

> So were the scores of once bustling towns and villages across the entire Greek world. The cultural losses were catastrophic and long lasting. For the next 450 years no monumental [large-scale] stone structures would be built in Greece. The art of writing was forgotten. . . . Centralized economic and political organization had disappeared along with the palaces [and] within a few generations all knowledge of those things disappeared, leaving only the memory of legendary warrior-chiefs, powerful rulers of once large and prosperous kingdoms, imagined as better men in every way than their puny descendants.

The Shift from Bronze to Iron

Historian Thomas R. Martin of the College of the Holy Cross, a Roman Catholic liberal arts college in Massachusetts, describes the beginnings of iron use in Greece during the Dark Age:

A significant shift in metallurgy [took] place throughout the Mediterranean region during the [900s and 800s] BCE—iron replac[ed] bronze as the principal metal used to make tools and weapons. [So] the Dark Age can also be referred to as the early Iron Age in Greece. Greeks probably learned the special metallurgical techniques needed to work iron . . . from traders searching for metal ores and [traveling] workers from Cyprus, Anatolia and the [Middle] East. Iron eventually replaced bronze, [especially] in the production of agricultural tools, swords, and spear points, although bronze remained in use for shields and armor. The use of iron spread because it offered practical advantages over bronze. For one thing, iron ore was relatively easy to procure, making iron tools and weapons less expensive than ones of bronze. Furthermore, iron implements kept their sharp edges longer because [iron] was harder than bronze.

Iron spear heads

Yet Greek civilization was far from dead. As the lost Minoan-Mycenaean civilization slipped into the realm of myths, small, isolated groups of people started to identify themselves with the valleys and islands they inhabited. Over time, these pockets of like-minded individuals became the cores of new political-social units known as city-states. When the Dark Age ended, giving way to the Archaic Age (ca. 800-ca. 500 BCE), these small states existed throughout the mainland, the Aegean islands, and the western coast of Anatolia, a Greek region that came to be called Ionia.

The Greek word for city-state was polis. An average polis consisted of a central urban center, or town, and several small villages and farms surrounding and supporting it. The urban center was most often built around a hill known as an acropolis, in Greek meaning "the city's high place." The most famous example is the Acropolis in Athens, which the city's residents fortified and fled to when intruders threatened. The Greek city-states had other similar features, such as outdoor marketplaces and temples erected to honor the gods that all Greeks recognized and worshiped. They also shared the Greek language and a rich heritage of myths from the Age of Heroes, their name for the lost era preceding the Dark Age. Despite these cultural similarities, however, the Greek states were passionately independent. They developed differing local customs and governments and came to see themselves as tiny separate nations.

As the Archaic Age progressed, numerous city-states enjoyed expanding commerce, including trade that ranged across the Mediterranean region. At the same time, writing revived. The new system employed an alphabet borrowed from a Middle Eastern maritime people, the Phoenicians. Another feature of the growing urban centers was large-scale architecture, at first applied to religious temples. These were initially made of wood but in late Archaic times the wood was replaced with stone. In addition, the period witnessed the rise of Panhellenic (all-Greek) shrines and athletic games, the most renowned at Olympia, in southwestern Greece; philosophy and scientific inquiry; and rapid colonization of the coasts of the Aegean, Black, and Mediterranean seas.

The Rise of Democracy

The coexistence of so many fiercely independent city-states and their vigorous economic expansion naturally led to disagreements among them, sometimes violent ones. This reality motivated the rise of local armies for defense. They came to be made up mainly of the small farmers who worked the lands surrounding the urban centers. These citizen militiamen, who assembled and fought only when needed, were heavily armored foot soldiers called hoplites. Employing thrusting spears, round shields, and short swords, they fought in a tightly packed battlefield formation known as a phalanx.

Because they held the military strength of a city-state, these tough, independent farmers felt little or no need to obey the orders of a handful of aristocrats living in the urban center. Before the hoplite revolution in the seventh century BCE, political power had been in the hands of such nobles. But the commoners, making up the bulk of the population, tended to resent them. As the hoplites and their phalanxes began to take shape, a few ambitious men in some larger cities took advantage of the situation. They got the citizen soldiers to support them and ruled as dictators. They came to be known as tyrants. Some were actually good leaders who promoted the arts and were popular with the masses.

As a form of government, however, tyranny lasted only a little more than a century in Greece. This was because the farmer-hoplites eventually concluded that they did not need dictators to rule them. Rather, they, along with other citizens, could choose any leaders they wanted by election. In the last century of the Archaic era, a steady movement toward democratic forms of government occurred in a number of city-states.

This trend produced its first and most significant outcome in Athens, located in the peninsula of Attica, in the south-central part of the Greek mainland. In the 590s BCE an Athenian statesman named Solon introduced several legal and political reforms. Among them were making fairer laws; giving expanded authority to an existing assembly of male citizens that until then had few powers; and allowing men of all social classes to serve as jurors in trials. Later, in about 508 BCE, another popular statesman, Cleisthenes, expanded on Solon's reforms, in the process creating the world's first true democracy. This milestone occurred at the dawn of what historians call Greece's Classical Age (ca. 500-323 BCE).

Laws Made by the People

The late historian Chester G. Starr, the author of more than twenty scholarly books on the history of the ancient world, described the core element of Cleisthenes's system—the new and improved *Ecclesia*, or Assembly:

Ideas were expressed directly in the Assembly, which consisted of all male citizens over 18 years of age who were willing to attend the sessions held about every 10 days. [In] this "direct democracy," whatever the people decided at the Assembly was the law. [Also] constitutional safeguards were built into the system. Any law passed by the Assembly had to be proposed by some one person, [and] if the citizens later thought they had made a mistake in passing it, they could attack the law in a court. . . . If the law was thus challenged within a year after its passage and found unconstitutional, its proposer was fined a sum that would bankrupt almost any citizen.

During the next few decades, other popular leaders, including Ephialtes and Pericles, introduced more reforms, making Athens's democracy increasingly expansive. In 431 BCE, at the zenith of his influence as a politician, Pericles could brag without exaggeration:

> Our constitution is called a democracy because power is in the hands not of a minority but of the whole people. When it is a question of settling private disputes, everyone is equal before the law, [and] no one, so long as he has it in him to be of service to the state, is kept in political obscurity because of poverty.

Athens's new and daring governmental system impressed many other Greeks. And in the fifth century BCE a number of other city-states fashioned their own versions of democracy. (Unfortunately, the details of how most of those governments worked have not survived.)

Rise of Imperial Athens

Partly because of its controversial adoption of democracy, Athens emerged in the fifth century BCE as one of Greece's most influential and prestigious states. Other factors in its ascension to power and glory included its large population (more than 300,000), extensive territory (almost 1,000 square miles), and its large fleets of merchant vessels and warships. Equally important was the leadership role the city played in fighting off foreign enemies. Greece was invaded twice in that century by armies of the Persian Empire which, centered in what are now Iran and Iraq, was the largest and most feared empire in the known world.

The first Persian incursion took place in 490 BCE. On the plain of Marathon, about twenty-six miles northeast of Athens, a force of 9,000 Athenian hoplites, aided by perhaps six hundred soldiers from the nearby tiny polis of Plataea, a longtime friend of Athens, faced a much larger enemy army. In a stunning turn of events, the Greeks crushed the invaders. More than 6,000 Persians died, compared to Athenian losses of only 192.

The second and much larger Persian assault occurred in 480 BCE. Led by the Persian king himself, Xerxes (ZERK-seez), a force of more than 200,000 troops entered Greece. This time many of the city-states united under Athens and its political rival, Sparta (situated about a hundred miles southwest of Athens). Just as Athens was known for its navy, Sparta was renowned for having the most feared land army in Greece. In a series of epic battles, the vastly outnumbered Greeks were once more victorious. After sustaining heavy losses, in 479 BCE the surviving Persians fled home, and their leaders never again attempted to invade Greece.

An illustration of King Xerxes of Persia circa 1553

The defeat of the world's greatest empire gave the Greeks a feeling of enormous accomplishment. They had shown the world, along with themselves, that they could do whatever they put their hearts and minds to. In the words of Canadian historian W. G. Hardy, beating the Persians became "the torch to set fire to the brilliance of the great age of the Greeks. There was a tremendous upswelling of confidence [and now they] felt that there was nothing they could not attempt."

That major injection of confidence led the Athenians to new economic, political, and artistic heights. They organized an alliance of more than a hundred city-states, the Delian League, with the goal of keeping Greece safe from further Persian attacks. However, the ambitious Athenians rapidly turned the alliance into their own extremely lucrative maritime empire. They used much of the wealth from the league's coffers to beatify their own city. Beginning in the 440s BCE, they constructed a spectacular temple complex atop the Acropolis. It was dominated by the Parthenon (dedicated to the city's patron, the goddess Athena). Pericles, who oversaw these projects, seemed to sense that he and his countrymen were creating something not just for their own time, but for all time. "The admiration of the present and succeeding ages will be ours," he stated, "since we have not left our power without witness, but have shown it by mighty proofs, [and] everywhere . . . have left imperishable monuments behind us."

War and Political Decline

The ambitious Athenians could not keep up such tremendous momentum indefinitely, however. The far more conservative Spartans, who had a powerful alliance of city-states of their own called the Peloponnesian League, balked at what they saw as Athenian arrogance, greed, and imperialism. In 431 BCE, the two blocs of Greek states entered a bloody contest for supremacy in Greece. Known as the Peloponnesian War, the conflict lasted for twenty-seven grueling years, and in the end proved ruinous for most of those involved. Reluctantly, the Athenians surrendered in 404 BCE. Their short-lived hegemony, or domination, of Greece was over, as was their equally brief golden age of architecture and other arts.

After its victory, through the early decades of the fourth century BCE, Sparta maintained its own hegemony of Greek affairs. However, the Spartans were poor politicians and administrators and were also tactless and awkward in dealing with other city-states. Because of their highly war-oriented ethos (cultural outlook), they tended to react to crises in a heavy-handed manner. In 382 BCE, for instance, civil strife erupted in Thebes, a city northeast of Athens, and Sparta reacted by sending troops to occupy the Theban urban center. Most Greeks strongly condemned the move.

A brief interlude of hope for more enlightened political management came when the Thebans, still seething over their humiliation by Sparta, rose to the challenge. Led by two talented statesmen-generals, Pelopidas and Epaminondas, Thebes reorganized its military. Then, in 371 BCE, it astonished the Greek world by soundly defeating the supposedly invincible Spartan phalanx.

Epaminondas, who took charge of the Theban hegemony of Greece that followed, was a fair and just individual. He hoped to bring the long-warring Greek states to some kind of general accord. But that unity was not to be. Many Greeks, including the Athenians and Spartans, opposed the Thebans, and the trend toward political anarchy and decline continued.

The Macedonian Hegemony

Close to a century of war and disunity had left the Greek states exhausted and weakened. Yet they remained blind to how susceptible they had become to attack from the outside. A brilliant young man named Philip was well aware of their vulnerability. He quietly began to draw his plans against them. As a prince of the kingdom of Macedonia, in extreme northern Greece, Philip knew a great deal about the drawbacks of disunity. Under a series of weak kings, the Macedonian tribes had long been disunited. That had made the kingdom militarily weak and relegated it to the status of a minor power on the fringes of the cultural sphere dominated by the strong southern city-states.

After ascending Macedonia's throne in 359 BCE, Philip united his country in only a few years. He created a strong standing army as well. Then, using an exceedingly efficient blend of diplomacy, deceit, and naked aggression, he seized much of northern and central Greece. Finally recognizing the threat he posed, Athens, Thebes, and several other leading states tried to block Philip's advance. But in 338 BCE at Chaeronea, northwest of Thebes, Philip easily crushed them on the battlefield. He then forced the city-states to join an alliance of states dominated by Macedonia.

Philip also told the city-states that they must supply troops for his planned invasion of the Persian Empire. However, Philip was not fated to achieve any more conquests. He was assassinated in 336 BCE and his son, Alexander III, who would later come to be called Alexander the Great, took charge of the Persian expedition.

Alexander the Great in battle, as depicted in this eighteenth-century relief inspired by Charles Le Brun's painting *The Battle of Gaugamela*

Two years later, Alexander led a small but powerful army from Greece into Anatolia, then a part of Persia, and defeated a group of Persian provincial governors. Not long afterward, he won two major victories over their king, Darius III. In only a decade Alexander managed to bring the Persian colossus to its knees and carve out an empire that stretched from Greece in the west to India in the east. Alexander had plans for more conquests, but he died prematurely, possibly of alcohol poisoning, in June 323. He was just a month or two shy of thirty-three.

A Man More than Human?

The ancient Greek historian Arrian, who wrote the most reliable ancient biography of Alexander, described him this way:

He had great personal beauty, invincible power of endurance, and a keen intellect [and] an uncanny instinct for the right course in a difficult and complex situation. . . . Noble indeed was his power of inspiring his men, of filling them with confidence [and] sweeping away their fear by the spectacle of his own fearlessness. . . . Never in all the world was there another like him, and therefore I cannot but feel that some power more than human was concerned in his birth.

A statue of Alexander the Great circa the third century BCE

The "Inhabited World"

Though huge in extent, Alexander's empire was one of the shortest-lived in history. Only months after his death, his leading generals and governors began quarreling, each aiming to take as much as he could of the vast domain. For forty years, these men and their sons, collectively called Alexander's "Successors," persistently opposed one another in a series of bloody conflicts and treacherous, shifting alliances.

Finally, around 280 BCE, three major new Greek political units existed in place of Alexander's former realm. The Seleucid Empire, founded by Seleucus, consisted of much of Iraq, Syria, and Anatolia; the Ptolemaic Kingdom, established by Ptolemy, encompassed Egypt and parts of nearby Palestine; and the Macedonian Kingdom, created by Antigonus Gonatas, consisted of Macedonia and sections of the Greek mainland. There were several smaller but influential kingdoms and city-states as well. Modern historians collectively call these realms Hellenistic, meaning "Greek-like." This is because their societies frequently featured traditional Eastern languages, customs, and ideas overlaid by a veneer of Greek ones. Similarly, scholars call the historical period starting with Alexander's death in 323 BCE and ending in 30 BCE Greece's Hellenistic Age.

During that era the Greek-ruled lands came to have remarkably similar social customs and political and economic institutions. As a result, the combined eastern Mediterranean region as well as the Middle East became a vast sphere with a common culture. Those who dwelled within it called it the *oikoumene* (ee-koo-MEH-nee), or "inhabited world." Its leading artists and scientists were extremely productive. Many worked in the Egyptian city of Alexandria, which had become the Greeks' chief commercial and intellectual center. Accomplishments were made in astronomy, anatomy, and other fields, while sculptors and painters achieved an unprecedented degree of detail and realism. This was part of a new trend toward a recognition of the worth of the individual person and concern for his or her needs.

Unfortunately for the Greeks, their common culture and scientific and social advances were not enough to ensure their security. In political and military matters they continued to repeat the same mistakes their ancestors had. In short, the Hellenistic states were almost constantly embroiled in wars with one another.

This disunity once more led to disaster. In 200 BCE, the Romans, masters of the Italian peninsula and recent conquerors of most of the western Mediterranean region, attacked and quickly defeated the Macedonian Kingdom. Even in the face of this major new threat, the other Greek states remained disunited. As a result, the Romans overcame them one by one. In 146 BCE, a Roman general ordered the complete destruction of one of Greece's leading cities, Corinth, to demonstrate the terrible price of further resistance.

No One Listened

The Ptolemaic Kingdom managed to remain nominally independent, although the Romans were ultimately in charge. They allowed the Ptolemies to conduct their own local affairs as long as they did what Rome wanted in the international sphere. It was understood that any non-cooperation might spell doom for the last major independent Greek state.

Indeed, the Ptolemaic queen Cleopatra VII discovered, to her extreme regret, how real that veiled threat was. In the 30s BCE she joined her lover, the powerful Roman Mark Antony, in a war against another powerful Roman, Octavian. The ill-fated lovers were disastrously defeated in a sea battle at Actium, in western Greece. Soon afterward they both committed suicide.

With Cleopatra's death, the last major Hellenistic domain became part of the growing Roman realm. Octavian went on to become Augustus, the first Roman emperor. Under his and his successors' rule, the Greeks retained their language and customs, but they were never again free (until the 1800s, when the modern nation of Greece was created).

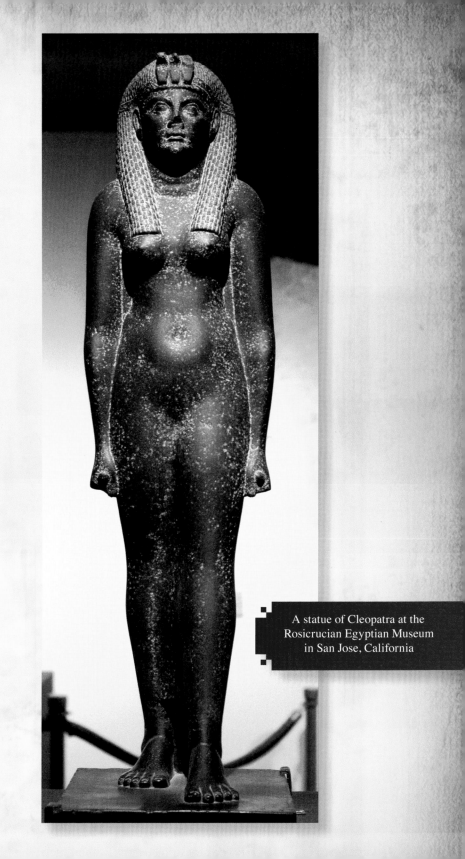

A statue of Cleopatra at the Rosicrucian Egyptian Museum in San Jose, California

Almost two centuries before this final humiliation, an orator named Agelaus of Aetolia had warned his fellow Greeks about the dangers of continued disunity. "It would be best of all if the Greeks never went to war with one another," he had said. Instead, they should "join hands like men who are crossing a river. In this way they could unite to repulse [their enemies] and to preserve themselves and their cities." Unfortunately, his advice went unheeded. And so, it was the Romans, and not the Greeks, who went on to bring together the far-flung peoples of the Mediterranean world into one vast empire.

Chapter Two:
Politics and Democracy

Fortunately for posterity, the Romans were captivated enough by a number of Greek artistic, religious, and other traditions to absorb them into their own culture. In the process they produced the hybrid Greco-Roman culture that has come to be called "Classical" civilization. When Rome disintegrated in the fifth and sixth centuries, many aspects of Greco-Roman culture passed on to later generations of Europeans. Thus, Greece's cultural legacy to modern Western civilization was not delivered directly by Greeks, but by Romans and medieval Europeans. In spirit and in facets of government, literature, athletics, and society too numerous to list, that legacy remains alive today.

Early Political Experiments
Some of the major cultural innovations the modern West inherited from the ancient Greeks were in the political and legal realm. In particular, democracy, which is today the most prevalent and desirable form of government in the world, was invented by the Greeks.

The ancient Greek city-states experimented widely with governmental systems and often varied in their approaches because they were in some ways separate peoples. No united Greek country, like today's Greece, existed in ancient times. What we think of as Ancient Greece was actually a collection of city-states that were small autonomous entities with varying political and social customs (although their citizens all spoke Greek and worshiped the same gods).

Many of these states fashioned their own versions of democracy between about 500 and 300 BCE. Regrettably, however, direct evidence explaining how most of these individual systems developed and functioned has not survived. The major exception is Athens. The most populous, ambitious, and cultured of the ancient Greek states, it was the first of them to develop democracy. It produced many major scholars and writers over the years, including the now famous Aristotle. He and others described the Athenian government of their era in detail, and many of their writings did survive. Evidence suggests that the other Greek states that adopted democracy were impressed by and to one degree or another copied the Athenian system. So an examination of that system will likely give at least a general idea of how most Greek democracies worked.

Like other Greek states, between about 800 and 750 BCE Athens emerged from a long period of poverty and illiteracy, Greece's so-called Dark Age. In the years that followed, it grew more prosperous and expanded its territory. Eventually it encompassed the entire Attic Peninsula, which juts outward into the Aegean Sea from the southeastern Greek mainland.

During these growth years, the Athenians also endured frequent political unrest and as a result experimented with different types of government. It appears that during the Dark Age the city's leader, like those of other Greek states, was called a basileus. Most early Greek writers referred to such leaders as kings. But as Sarah B. Pomeroy, a distinguished professor of classics and history at Hunter College in New York City, points out:

It would be misleading [to] call the Dark Age leaders "kings," a title that conjures up in the modern mind visions of monarchs with autocratic powers. A more appropriate name for the Dark Age basileus is the [term] "chief," which suggests a man with far less power than a king. The basileus, nevertheless, was a man of great stature and importance in his community.

A Series of Reforms

At some point in the 700s BCE, the Athenians decided to replace their chief with a council made up of three public administrators called archons. They were all aristocrats, or of noble birth. So it is entirely possible that the man who would normally have served as basileus now sat with two peers on the council.

Initially, the three archons served for life. But in the early 600s BCE they began to be chosen on an annual basis by election. Soon after that, moreover, the number of archons on the council was raised to nine. As for who voted these men into office, the general consensus of scholars is that it was a group of Athenian landowners who met periodically in a gathering called the Ecclesia, or Assembly. At the time, that group seems to have had no other powers of any consequence.

On leaving office, an archon joined a larger, highly esteemed council called the Areopagus. (It was named for the hill of that name on which its members met. The Areopagus rose only a few hundred feet from Athens's central, fortified hill, the Acropolis.) Exactly what the members of the Areopagus did in this period is unclear. They may have advised or prepared the yearly agenda (list of issues to deal with) for the archons.

In any case, all of the men in both governing bodies were aristocrats. Having control of the legal system, they often passed laws that mainly benefited themselves, a practice the common people came to deeply resent. Eventually, some sort of public pressure forced the nobles to change the system.

In the late 600s they appointed a man named Draco to craft a written list of laws that members of all social classes must follow. The people viewed these new laws as much too harsh, however, which must have generated more protests. By the early 500s BCE, Athens was on the verge of a violent social revolution.

Fortunately for the city, no bloody insurrection occurred. In 594 BCE, the opposing factions asked a citizen known for his wisdom and fairness to negotiate a compromise. His name was Solon. After much deliberation, he proposed what were seen at the time as very radical legal and social reforms. First, he threw out Draco's oppressive laws, except for those dealing with murder. He also created a new social ranking based on wealth rather than birth. That made it possible for commoners who managed to accumulate a certain amount of money to be elected to the office of archon.

In addition, Solon introduced the Boule, or Council, a group of four hundred men chosen from all social classes by lot (random drawing). Each man served for a year. So there was a good chance that nearly every Athenian man would serve at least once in his life. The Council's job was to draw up an agenda for the Assembly, which now had more authority. Thanks to Solon, the Council and Assembly now balanced the influence of the aristocratic Areopagus.

Solon's Strong Shield

Solon left behind writings that described his political reforms. He said in part:

To the people I have given just as much power as suffices, neither taking away from their due [rights], nor offering more. While for those who had power and were honored for wealth, I have taken thought likewise, that they should suffer nothing unseemly. I stand [guard] with [a] strong shield flung around both parties, and have allowed neither to win an unjust victory.

A copper engraving of Solon, the Athenian statesman (left)

Full Democracy and the Assembly

The most enduring and momentous of Solon's reforms was giving ordinary Athenians, including people of modest means, a real voice in government. This was a political advance that had never occurred anywhere else in the world up to that time. And it opened the way for the development of full-blown democracy.

That historic event took place fewer than nine decades later. In 508 BCE, an Athenian nobleman named Cleisthenes found himself in a power struggle with some opposing aristocrats. Unlike his more arrogant rivals, he was not against sharing power with the lower classes. He also understood the political potential of persuading the commoners to take his side. In a brilliant move, he offered them an expanded role in government in return for their support. In the words of the fifth-century BCE Greek historian Herodotus (later called the "father" of history), Cleisthenes "took the people into his party."

The late, noted historian Michael Grant called the new political system introduced by Cleisthenes "the most democratic form of government that had so far been devised by human ingenuity." In fact, it was the world's first true democracy. Operated by people from all social classes, it was based on a principle the Greeks called *isonomia*, meaning "equality under the law."

This political equality was most obvious in the workings of the new version of the Assembly, which now had substantial powers. Besides directly electing some public officials, it alone—not the nobles—had the authority to declare war. Moreover, the assembled citizens decided a conflict's overall strategy, how many soldiers or ships would be used, and which generals would be in charge. In addition, the Assembly possessed the sole authority to make peace, grant citizenship, establish colonies, distribute public money for local construction projects, and decide foreign policy. No other group of citizens in history, including those in the most open modern democracies, has ever exerted so much direct political clout.

Other Aspects of Democracy

One way the Athenian system differed from those in modern democracies was the manner in which it defined the term *citizen*. Only free males born in Attica had full citizenship rights in the new democracy, including the political rights of voting and holding public office. Athenian women were also citizens. However, they were a special kind known as *astai*, meaning those *without* political rights. Excluded completely from

Loss of Citizenship

Full citizenship in Athens's democracy was a special and highly coveted right. Having one's citizenship revoked, called *atimia*, was viewed as a tremendous loss and hardship. A man who had lost his citizenship, usually for committing a serious crime, was known as an *atimos*. He was barred from speaking in the Assembly or law courts. Nor could he hold public office or even walk into a temple or the marketplace. Any citizen who saw an *atimos* in these or other forbidden areas had the authority to arrest him and turn him over to the authorities.

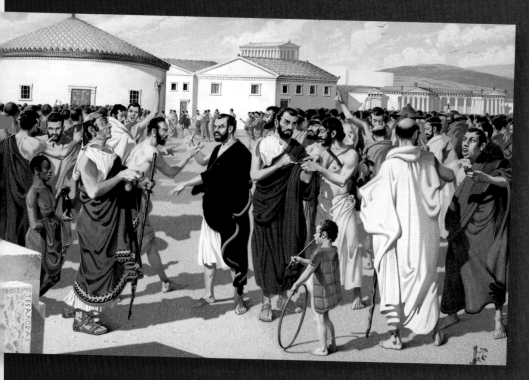

A painting of men voting to ostracize a fellow citizen in the Athenian Agora

citizenship were slaves (who had no legal rights) and metics. The latter were foreigners who lived and worked in Athens. They included both non-Greeks and Greeks from other city-states. (The metics were mainly merchants and artisans, such as potters and jewelers. Though not citizens, they did pay taxes and serve in the military if they were needed.)

Another existing institution that underwent major reform in the new democratic government was the Council. Its membership increased from four to five hundred. And its functions expanded as well, as explained by archaeologist Lesley Adkins:

> The Council prepared all proposals [for new laws] for the Assembly and implemented decisions of the Assembly (which were delegated to boards of officials). It also received embassies [visiting foreign officials] and undertook the everyday affairs of the state, such as controlling public finance and administering public buildings. It was responsible for certain religious cults and sacrifices and had some judicial [court-related] functions.

Still another important aspect of the new democracy was the *strategia*, a board of ten generals (*strategoi*) elected by the Assembly. The generals, who, like councilors, served for a year, were more than just military commanders. They regularly addressed the Assembly, proposed new laws and state policies, and could even call for a special meeting of the Assembly. The generals also carried out that body's foreign policy programs. In some ways an Athenian general resembled a modern democratic president; only Athens had ten of them instead of one at any given time.

Also like modern presidents, the generals were sometimes popular and sometimes not. If he was popular, a general might be reelected to several more one-year terms, in which case he could become an extremely influential and powerful statesman. The most famous example was Pericles. Elected *strategos* more than twenty times (fifteen of them consecutively), he guided Athens to its zenith of power and artistic splendor in the mid-400s BCE.

The Athenian democrats also built into their system the means of removing a general or other public official who became too ambitious or abused his authority. One safeguard lay among the Assembly's large array of powers. Its members could fine an offensive official, remove him from office, or even condemn him to death. Another security feature was a procedure known as ostracism. Each citizen scratched onto a piece of broken pottery called an *ostracon* the name of the person he felt should be removed from office. If 6,000 of these negative votes were cast, the official lost his position. He was also banished from Athens for ten years, although he retained his property and citizenship.

A terracotta ostracon bearing the name Themistocles, from the fifth century BCE. Ostracons were used when there was a fear of tyranny, to ostracize politicians considered dangerous for democracy.

Democracy in Later Ages

It appears that Athens's democratic institutions (and possibly those of some other Greek states) remained in place for sometime after the Romans conquered Greece in the second century BCE. However, these democracies disappeared during the early years of the Roman Empire (30 BCE-476 CE). Thereafter, no true democratic governments existed in the world until the United States' founding fathers, inspired in part by ancient Athenian democracy, established their new nation in 1776. In turn, in the two centuries that followed other peoples created their own versions of democracy. As a result, in 2009, of the world's 194 nations, 89 were fully democratic and another 58 partly democratic. It is therefore fair to say that, at least politically speaking, the ancient Greeks were far ahead of their time.

Chapter Three:
Philosophy and Science

A group of Greek thinkers were the first people to fashion a systematic, or deliberate and orderly, approach to science. When they made their earliest scientific proposals in the 600s and 500s BCE, these thinkers described themselves as philosophers. In later ages, philosophy came to be seen as the effort to define ethical concepts such as virtue and justice. But in the seventh century BCE the discipline of philosophy also included what are now defined as scientific concepts. Science and philosophy had not yet divided into separate fields of inquiry. These early Greek thinkers later came to be called the pre-Socratics because they came before the fifth-century BCE Athenian philosopher Socrates. Having no interest in science, he confined himself to ethical inquiry, launching the study of philosophy as separate from scientific investigation.

Searching for Nature's First-Principle

The birth date of the first important pre-Socratic thinker, Thales, is unknown. But it appears that he was active in the early 500s BCE.

Thales attempted to explain the workings of nature without resorting to gods, spirits, demons, and other supernatural beings and powers. This approach, utilized by all the Greek scientists who followed, immediately separated them from thinkers in Egypt, Babylonia, and other foreign lands. The latter had long believed that supernatural forces determined nature's course, including human life and endeavors. But Thales and his Greek successors instead viewed the universe, or cosmos, as a rational, ordered domain that operated on underlying scientific principles. Moreover, they argued that humans had the mental capacity to discover and explain those principles.

To that end, Thales began searching for what he and other Greek scientists called the *physis* (from which the term "physics" derives). They defined it as nature's fundamental physical principle, or the substance underlying all matter that could be seen and touched. Thales eventually concluded that the physis was water. A later Greek thinker, Theophrastus, explained his predecessor's thinking this way:

> Warmth lives in moisture. Moreover, the seeds as well as the nourishment of things are moist. And it is natural that what gives birth to a thing should also be its means of nourishment. Since water is the first-principle of the moistness of anything, [Thales] declares it to be the first-principle of everything.

A number of other Greek thinkers disagreed that water was nature's first-principle. One of them was a student of Thales—Anaximander. In Anaximander's opinion, the physis was an everlasting, unchanging, and unseen material that he called the "Boundless." He claimed that nature's main elements—earth, water, air, and fire—had been manufactured within or by the Boundless.

Also, in a different but no less important scientific vein, Anaximander suggested that the first living creatures arose from the sea. These creatures eventually crawled out onto the dry land, he said, and adapted themselves to their new environment. This basic and largely correct description of evolution predated modern evolutionary scientists, including Charles Darwin, by more than twenty-five centuries.

A later Greek thinker, Anaxagoras, proposed still another hypothesis for the nature of the physis. The tiny "seeds" of all the tangible substances on earth exist deep inside all things, he proposed. To illustrate this somewhat mystifying idea, Anaxagoras called attention to the act and consequences of eating. When people consume bread, fruits, and vegetables, he pointed out, they grow bones, skin, and hair. This could only happen, he contended, if the seeds of bones, skin, and hair already existed in the food when it was eaten. He wrote:

> For how [else] could hair come from what is not hair, or flesh from what is not flesh? In everything there is a portion of everything else, [which means that] nothing exists apart. . . . When all things were together, before any separating had taken place, not even any color was discernible. This was because of the utter mixture of all things—of moist with dry, hot with cold, bright with dark.

What are the Sun and Milky Way?

Although he is best known today for his theory about tiny seeds lying inside all substances, Anaxagoras appears to have been most interested in the heavenly bodies. This short summary of his astronomical ideas was penned by the third-century Greco-Roman scholar Diogenes Laertius.

[When] asked to what end he had been born, [Anaxagoras] replied, "To study sun, and moon, and heavens." [He] declared the sun to be a mass of red-hot metal. [He also] declared that there were dwellings on the moon, and moreover hills and ravines. [In addition, Anaxagoras] held the Milky Way to be a reflection of the light of stars which are not shown upon by the sun, [and] comets to be a conjunction [coming together] of planets which emit flames.

The Greek Astronomers

It is notable that Anaxagoras's primary scientific interest was astronomy. Many Greek thinkers, both before and after Socrates, expressed similar curiosity about the natures of the sun, planets, and stars and their connections to earth. For instance, Anaximander suggested that the stars were hoops of fire that had been compressed by air.

A similar theory was proposed by Heraclitus, who flourished about 500 BCE. He was also the first-known scientist to recognize that the stars are other suns. According to Diogenes Laertius, Heraclitus said that "the other stars are further from the earth [than the sun is] and for that reason give it less light and heat." Still another pre-Socratic Greek thinker, Philolaus, correctly labeled earth a planet, like Venus, Jupiter, and Mars.

He also rightly said that earth orbits a central fire. What made his theory different from reality was his assertion that said central fire was separate from the sun. In his cosmic view, both earth and the sun revolved around the central fire.

Most post-Socratic Greek philosopher-scientists preferred the idea of a geocentric, or earth-centered universe. Among them was the highly influential Athenian scholar Plato. In addition to his now famous writings about law, politics, and ethics, he produced the *Timaeus*, a broad depiction of the cosmos and the heavenly bodies existing within it. Some modern scientists see the *Timaeus* as the first important work of cosmology, the branch of astronomy dealing with the universe's origins.

Like most Greek thinkers before him, Plato declared that earth was a sphere lying at the center of all things. He also held that both the universe and time had long ago come into being in an instant, "in order that, having been created together, if ever there was to be a dissolution of them, they might be dissolved together." This idea loosely resembles the current thinking of most astronomers. Called the "big bang" theory, it suggests that the universe suddenly began expanding from a tiny central point close to 14 billion years ago. And time, as humans know it, began at the same instant.

A herm of Plato on display at the Altes Museum in Berlin, Germany

Plato's brilliant student Aristotle, also an Athenian, agreed that earth was a sphere located at the center of the universe. Part of his proof for a spherical earth was his observation that its shadow on the moon's face during a lunar eclipse is curved. Aristotle was right about earth's shape. But his acceptance of the geocentric view was wrong. And because late medieval and early modern Europeans saw Aristotle and his ideas as practically infallible, that earth-centered view was widely accepted for almost two thousand years.

The only ancient scientist who got earth's position in the universe right was Aristarchus of Samos. A Greek scholar who worked in a university-like institution in Alexandria, Egypt, he argued that earth and the other planets orbited the sun. Most of Aristarchus's writings did not survive. And unfortunately, his heliocentric, or sun-centered, vision was largely rejected by the majority of scientists and educated people, who slavishly followed Aristotle. (In the 1500s, Polish astronomer Nicolas Copernicus revived the heliocentric theory, marking the birth of modern astronomy. Shortly before publishing his masterwork, Copernicus acknowledged his debt to Aristarchus.)

Other Scientific Efforts

Aristotle's enormous influence as a thinker and scientist was not confined to astronomy. He also made major strides in the still-forming disciplines of biology and zoology. One of his most important accomplishments was the invention of an efficient scheme for classifying animals. In addition, he collected thousands of animal specimens and studied them in detail.

In so doing, he established the earliest versions of the biological fields of embryology (growth in the womb), comparative anatomy, and ecology (animals' connection to the environment). In recognition of these efforts, modern scientists came to call him the "father" of biology.

Simply listing the other Greek scientists of Aristotle's day and the four to five centuries that followed would fill several pages. Among the more outstanding and famous examples was Theophrastus. He laid the foundations for the science of botany, the study of the plant kingdom, and was later called the "father" of botany. Meanwhile, Democritus and Leucippus expounded the first atomic theory. In their search for nature's physis, they proposed, correctly it turned out, that all matter is composed of tiny, invisible particles called atoms.

Other Greek thinkers became doctors and medical researchers. Hippocrates (fifth century BCE), the "father" of medicine, penned numerous treatises on surgery, anatomy, diseases of women and children, and medical ethics. Herophilus and his student Erasistratus expanded knowledge of anatomy, including descriptions of the human digestive organs and the motor and sensory nerves.

Still other Greek scientists established the field of mechanics. Strato studied the phenomena of force and motion and explained how moving objects accelerate. His younger contemporary, Archimedes, derived the mathematical formulas for the volumes of spheres and cylinders and experimented with

Why No Greek Industrial Revolution?

It is natural to wonder why the Greek scientists who established the field of mechanics did not create elaborate work-saving devices like those of the Industrial Revolution of the 1700s and 1800s. They were certainly clever enough. (For example, Ctesibius fashioned simple pistons and Hero made a small steam engine.) There were two principal reasons why no ancient Greek industrial revolution occurred. First, ancient metal-working techniques were incapable of producing machine parts of sufficient strength and accuracy. Second, the wealthy ruling classes, whose money would have been needed to finance large-scale industry, felt no need or desire for work-saving machines. This was because they already had all the cheap labor they required in the form of slaves.

levers, pulleys, and other simple machines. In the same century, Ctesibius (t'SIB-ee-us) developed the simple cylinder and plunger, used later in thousands of machines, including car engines. Later, another Greek thinker, Hero, built a small steam engine.

Reshaping Western Thought

While Anaxagoras, Democritus, Hippocrates, and their colleagues were building the foundations for most of the major scientific disciplines, Socrates was doing the same for philosophy. An odd-looking little man who dressed like a pauper, he wandered the streets of Athens and stopped passersby at random. Typically he challenged them to examine their lives and asked them if they understood and lived by ethical principles such as goodness and justice. He became a sort of promoter of virtue and searcher for life's ultimate truths. At the time, he likely did not foresee that he was establishing a moral philosophy that would later reshape Western thought.

Socrates realized that to properly define goodness and other ethical concepts one had first to examine them closely under varying circumstances. No organized method for doing so then existed. So he invented one—his interviews with his fellow citizens. In each case he asked a series of insightful questions about a subject, claiming that he was ignorant of the answers. The responses the person gave him often led to the truth of the subject, or at least an approximation of it. This form of inquiry and learning later came to be called the "Socratic method" in his honor. Plato, who in his youth was a close friend and follower, later remarked that a person who conversed at length with Socrates was "continually carried round

Italian painter Raphael's *The School of Athens*, circa 1505, shows several Greek philosophers including Plato (center left), Aristotle (center right), and Socrates (to the left of Plato in the brownish-green robe)

and round by him, until at last he [found] that he [had] to give an account both of his present and past life. And when he [was] once entangled, Socrates [would] not let him go until he [had] completely and thoroughly sifted him."

Socrates left no writings of his own. So all that is known about his thinking comes from the writings of Plato and a few others. Plato wrote how he was emotionally crushed when the Athenian government tried and executed his mentor on the false charge of corrupting the city's young people.

The younger man eventually came to devote much of his time to exploring the same ethical concepts Socrates had. Plato, too, tried to define goodness, justice, and truth. And his numerous writings motivated later generations of Western thinkers to deliberate similarly. Many centuries later, the English philosopher Alfred North Whitehead famously quipped that the entire Western philosophical tradition was basically "a series of footnotes to Plato." Although this was a purposeful exaggeration, the contributions that Socrates and Plato made to the developing field of philosophy were nothing short of enormous. Indeed, all later Western thinkers either accepted and absorbed their ideas or felt obligated to clarify why they differed with them.

Chapter Four:
Theaters, Plays, and Acting

Almost everyone in modern developed countries such as the United States enjoys popular forms of entertainment such as plays, movies, and television comedies and dramas. But very few people are aware of where the basis for all such entertainment—the theater—came from. As is true of so many Western cultural traditions, the theater was invented by the ancient Greeks. More specifically, it sprang into existence and reached its height of ancient splendor in a single city and in the amazingly brief period of a few decades. That city was Athens, which experienced its famous cultural golden age in the fifth century BCE. In that short but pivotal interlude, a handful of talented individuals created the model for great theater and drama for all times.

Performers for Dionysus

Modern scholars are somewhat uncertain about the exact origins of Greek theater and drama. But evidence suggests that they developed from a special set of religious rituals performed in many ancient Greek city-states. Those ceremonies honored Dionysus, god of fertility, the vine, and the vine's main product, wine. During such a ceremony, a group of worshipers sang and danced to sacred verses collectively known as dithyramb. The words of said verses told the traditional tale of Dionysus's life and exploits. Through their songs and moves, those specially trained worshipers brought to life episodes from the myths associated with the god. In a very real sense, they were performers and their fellow worshipers who watched them were their audience.

As time went on, in Athens and possibly elsewhere, these highly dramatic and moving rites grew larger and more elaborate and included the stories of other gods. Probably by the early 500s BCE they also dramatized the adventures of a few popular mythical human heroes. It was in Athens that sometime later in that century the priests who led the rituals started enhancing the dithyrambic verses by adding, deleting, or otherwise altering them.

Aristotle on the Dithyramb

The great fourth-century BCE Athenian scholar Aristotle discussed the origins of theater in his treatise *Poetics*:

It certainly began in improvisations [inventions] originating with the authors of the dithyramb . . . which still survive as institutions in many of our cities. And its advance [development] after that was little by little, through their improving on whatever they had before them at each stage. It was in fact only after a long series of changes that the [evolution] of [drama] stopped [after] attaining its [present] form.

Key Early Innovations

A major transition from the Dionysian rituals to actual theater occurred in 534 BCE. That year Athens initiated a new annual religious festival dedicated to Dionysus. Known appropriately as the City Dionysia, its main attraction was a contest in which several men vied to write the most artful and appealing version of dithyramb. The winner of the competition was a person named Thespis. A talented individual, in subsequent contests he experimented with a number of new ideas in an effort to make his presentations stand out. (In honor of his key contributions to the theater, modern actors are sometimes called "thespians.")

In one of these innovations, he *pretended to be* a god or hero instead of simply *telling about* that character. To carry this off, he stepped away from the singers and dancers—by this time called the chorus—and exchanged lines with them. That made him the first known actor in history. Moreover, the exchange of dialogue made his newest entry in the contest the first known play.

This fresh approach to telling the well-known stories of gods and heroes became popular. As a result, Thespis and his competitors kept on experimenting. Someone—it might or might not have been Thespis—got the idea of having the single actor play more than one character in the same story. To distinguish one character from another required disguises. And this led to the use of masks, one for each character, which thereafter became a standard convention of Greek theater. At some point the members of the chorus also started wearing masks. Usually they were identical, so as, in scholar Iris Brooke's words, "to represent a community without any individuality." That made the lone actor's character stand out more. Brooke, the author of more than twenty books on historical costumes, goes on to tell what the masks looked like:

They not only covered the face, but carried the ornate [elaborate] hair styles or headdress peculiar to the part played by the actor at that particular time. Thus a woman would appear with her hair dressed [nicely] if she were meant to represent a woman in fashion, or with her hair [cut short] if she were a character in mourning [or] with a crown [if] she were a queen.

A theater mask dating from the fourth to third centuries BCE on display at the Ancient Agora Museum in Athens

Play Production in Athens

At first, Thespis and his successors continued to base their stories and characters on those in mythology. But eventually a few began to turn to historical events for material. The fifth-century Greek historian Herodotus told how the playwright Phrynichus caused a stir in the great festival in 492 BCE. The play was *The Capture of Miletus*, describing that important Greek city's seizure by the Persians (based in what are now Iran and Iraq). The play was so disturbing to the spectators, Herodotus said, that they "burst into tears. The author was fined a thousand drachmas for reminding them of a disaster which touched them so closely, and they forbade anybody ever to put the play on the stage again."

By the time *The Capture of Miletus* was banned, Athens's drama festival was a large-scale cultural event that attracted both Athenians and people from neighboring Greek cities. It was held in March and lasted several days. Hoping to advertise the city's growing reputation as an artistic center and wealthy state, the government paid for some of the expenses. First, it built and maintained the building where the plays were staged—the Theatre in Dionysus. Carved into the southeastern base of the Acropolis, it was at first made of wood and packed earth. But in later renovations the wood was replaced by stone, and it attained a seating capacity of 14,000.

The Athenian government also paid the actors. However, other aspects of play production, including sets, costumes, musicians, and training the choruses were financed by well-to-do Athenians. These backers were known as *choregoi*. The playwrights also had duties beyond writing the stories, including overseeing rehearsals, composing the music, and choreographing the dances.

Another responsibility of the playwright was decorating the outer wall of the *skene*. This "scene building," situated behind the orchestra (the circular area where the acting took place), was an enclosure that tripled as prop storage, actors' dressing room, and scenic backing for the plays. Along with some helpers, the playwright painted on it an appropriate landscape, street scene, or other setting appropriate to the story. The rest of the settings were left to the spectators' imaginations.

The props stored in the skene and used in the shows included couches, torches, statues of gods, swords, and a few other basic objects to enhance the onstage action. There were also a few mechanical devices to provide what would today be called "special effects." One popular one was the *eccyclema*, or "tableau machine," a platform with little wheels at the bottom. Murders nearly always happened offstage. So sometimes an onstage moment of horror was created when stagehands pushed the eccyclema into view. On it stood the murderer and victim, frozen in a snapshot-like pose depicting the moment of the bloody deed.

Tragedy and Aeschylus

Like modern playwrights, those who worked in fifth-century BCE Athens varied in quality. Usually only the best were chosen to compete in the City Dionysia. The city's cultural golden age produced dozens of extremely talented dramatists, but the only complete plays that have survived are those of the four giants of the era. Of these, three wrote tragedies. They were mostly serious stories that explored the various ways that evil or human shortcomings caused unhappiness and misery. Journalist and author David Sacks elaborates:

> Greek tragedy drew on tales from myth. This meant that in most cases the entire audience would be familiar with the story's plot beforehand (similar to a modern audience at an Easter pageant). . . . Most Greek tragedy presents the downfall of a hero or other lofty [character]. This downfall is [frequently] shown to be due to hubris (arrogance). Having attracted the anger of the gods, the hero is destroyed by a disastrously arrogant decision of his own.

From the standpoint of the audience, tragedy was not just entertainment. It was also a way for the spectators to purge, or vent, their pent-up frustrations, a process called catharsis. In a famous passage from his *Poetics*, Aristotle said that tragedy should depict "incidents arousing pity and fear, [in order] to accomplish its catharsis of such emotions."

The first of the three Athenian giants of tragedy, Aeschylus, was a master at creating catharsis. He wrote eighty-two plays, but only seven survive complete. They include the *Persians*, depicting the Persian Empire's invasion of Greece eight years before; and the Oresteia trilogy, consisting of *Agamemnon*, *The Libation Bearers*, and *The Eumenides*, showing a noble family ravaged by a curse. Aeschylus reportedly won first prize in the festival competition thirteen times.

Aeschylus also introduced the convention of a second actor. With only a single actor there could be only a few characters, since he could exit and reenter wearing a new mask only so many times. That also limited the complexity of the stories. Having two actors allowed for more characters and more elaborate stories.

Sophocles and Euripides

Aeschylus's younger colleague, Sophocles, went even further and utilized a third actor. He not only enlarged the storytelling potential of drama, but also became a master of character portrayal. Many of his main characters possess a serious defect in personality or attitude, later termed a "tragic flaw." This imperfection typically brings about much suffering as well as the character's own downfall.

Sophocles was reportedly the most successful playwright ever to enter the City Dionysia, winning it eighteen times. He was also incredibly prolific, turning out 123 plays. Seven have survived, including *Antigone*, *Electra*, and *Oedipus the King*. The latter was his most renowned work, one that some drama critics have called the greatest tragedy ever written.

In the story, based on a popular myth, Oedipus is king of Thebes. Unknowingly, he fulfills a horrifying prophecy that had warned he would slay his father and marry his mother. Discovering what he has done, he screams in agony and gouges out his own eyes.

The third giant of tragedy, Euripides, wrote about eighty-eight plays, of which nineteen have survived. Among them are *Medea*, *Hippolytus*, and the *Madness of Heracles*. Euripides quite often questioned traditional social values. He also tended to depict the gods in unflattering ways. In his play *Ion*, for example, he had the god Apollo rape a female character, who then condemned that divinity. Athenian audiences initially viewed both of these acts as offensive. As a result, Euripides was not as popular as Sophocles and Aeschylus in their time. Only in later ages did people come to appreciate Euripides's use of frankness and realism in exploring the human condition.

A Tribute to Humanity

Sophocles viewed humans as imperfect creatures. Yet he also felt they had some good qualities and that under the right circumstances they had the potential for greatness. He paid tribute to his fellow humans in an often-cited passage from his play *Antigone*:

Many wonders exist, but none of them are more wonderful than human beings. . . . They have taught themselves to speak and think quickly and to create communities. . . . Clever beyond one's wildest dreams are the abilities that cause them sometimes to do evil and other times to do good. As long as they respect the rule of law and the authority of the gods, their community will proudly continue to thrive.

The Old Comedy

Another dramatist who was often controversial in his day was the master of comedy, Aristophanes. He was said to have produced forty-four plays. Of these, eleven have survived, among them *Clouds*, *Birds*, *Lysistrata*, and *Frogs*.

An illustration of a scene from Aristophanes's *Birds*

Aristophanes was popular during a period that later scholars came to call the "Old Comedy," lasting from about 450 to 404 BCE. He and other comic playwrights employed topical humor that satirized, or poked fun at, politicians, military generals, and other prominent members of the community. There was also much dirty language, sexual innuendo, and vulgar slap-stick humor. For a while Athens was the only place in which artists could get away with such frank expression because its democracy guaranteed freedom of speech.

Aristophanes also had the sad distinction of reaching his height of popularity at a time of extreme national crisis. A year after *Frogs* appeared, Athens was defeated in the ruinous Peloponnesian War, and its cultural golden age ended. The dramatic festivals continued, but the tremendous level of innovation and creative output they had witnessed in the fifth century BCE was never again attained.

Nevertheless, over the centuries the theater and its conventions spread far and wide. As one modern scholar aptly puts it, ancient Greek drama "was in many ways the hallmark of Athenian greatness. Through Shakespeare and other great [playwrights] of Europe, this remarkable [cultural achievement] forms an important part of a legacy that has endured to our own time."

Chapter Five:
Poetry and Other Literature

Western society's literary heritage from ancient Greece is enormous. The Greeks produced not only the first examples of European literature but went on to invent almost every major literary form in use in the modern world. Among others, they include political, philosophical, scientific, and ethical treatises, historical works, tragic and comic plays, literary reviews, oratorical prose (speech-writing), and prose fiction, including the novel. Moreover, though the Greeks did not invent poetry, they utilized every poetic genre and produced a huge output of high-quality works in each.

Indeed, quality—including inventiveness and excellence of execution—was a hallmark of Greek literature. So was a penetrating insight into human nature and the practical problems and spiritual yearnings inherent in both ancient and modern societies. As the late, English classical scholar C. M. Bowra pointed out:

The most striking quality of Greek literature, poetry and prose alike, is that it is as
alive and relevant today as it was when it was
first written. We cannot fail to respond to the
extraordinary power with which it presents
issues of perennial urgency. We may admire
it for its technical skill, but what binds us to it
is its profound humanity [and] its wise appre-
ciation of human values. It deals with precise
issues in a universal way, [and] its extraordinary immediacy and directness drive home
its imaginative thoughts with an irresistible
power.

Epic Poems

One would expect that the literary "technical skill" Bowra
mentioned would take a while to develop. It would therefore
be logical to assume that the earliest Greek literary works
were crude or amateurish and improved over time. But
that was not the case. The very first examples of Western
literature were the epic poems the *Iliad* and the *Odyssey*,
attributed to the eighth-century BCE poet Homer. Despite
the fact that they appeared when the Greeks were just learning the art of writing, they were literary masterpieces of
surpassing power, insight, and technical prowess.

This seemingly implausible situation begins to make
sense when one examines the unusual manner in which
these works were created. As talented a writer as Homer
undoubtedly was, he probably did not compose the works
by himself. Rather, they began as oral traditions centuries
before. That is, poets called bards recited early versions
of the works from memory and passed them on to later
generations. Bards in each succeeding generation added
to and refined them. So by the time Homer received them,
they were likely to have been of considerable quality.
It appears that his contribution was to give them their most

Homer recounting the deeds of the Bronze Age Greeks in the Trojan War, as portrayed in this hand-colored reproduction of a nineteenth-century illustration

extensive refinement yet. Then either he or a younger contemporary dictated them to someone who wrote them down, which ended their oral evolution and froze them in a more or less permanent form.

The two works thereafter captured the imaginations of each new generation of ancient Greeks. They were thrilled by the exploits of the heroes in the *Iliad*, about the pivotal events of the last year of the legendary Trojan War. And they were fascinated by the Cyclops (one-eyed giant) and other monsters in the *Odyssey*, which recalls the wanderings of the Greek warrior Odysseus. More than mere entertainment, however, Homer's epics had a profound effect on Greek society and thought. In the words of historian Michael Grant, they furnished the Greeks with "their greatest civilizing influence, and formed the foundation of their literary, artistic, moral, social, educational, and political attitudes. [They] attracted universal esteem and reverence, too, as sources of general and practical wisdom, [and] as mines of endless quotations and commentaries, the common property of Greeks everywhere."

Homer was not the only Greek epic poet. Many epics were written in the centuries that followed him, but a majority are now lost. However, their existence is known because of surviving fragments and/or descriptions of them by later Greek writers who had read them. Particularly impressive was the Epic Cycle, a group of long poems dealing with the mythical ages preceding the rise of the Greek city-states. One of these was the *Titanomachy*, about a legendary war between two races of gods, the Titans and Olympians. Three other early epics—the *Oedipodea*, *Thebaïs*, and *Epigoni*—contained stories relating to the founding and early rulers of the city of Thebes. Still other lost epics described incidents surrounding the Trojan War that did not appear in Homer's epics, including the *Sack of Troy* and *Little Iliad*.

One early epic poet—a young man when Homer was old—wrote two epic poems that did survive. He was a farmer named Hesiod. Believing that some minor goddesses known as Muses had inspired him, he composed an epic about the creation of the world and early exploits of the gods. He titled the work, based partly on the then existing *Titanomachy*, the *Theogony* ("the ancestry of the gods"). Hesiod's other epic is the *Works and Days*, which extols the merits of working hard and running one's farm in the most proper and efficient ways possible.

Stop Being a Lazy Drone!

In this passage from his *Works and Days*, Hesiod scolds his lazy brother, Perses, and urges him to work harder or else suffer starvation:

Remember what I keep telling you over and over— work, O Perses . . . so that famine will avoid you [and] Demeter [goddess of grain crops] will be your friend, and fill your barn with [the] substance of living. Famine is the unworking man's most constant companion. Gods and men alike resent that man who, without work[ing] himself, lives the life of the stingless drone, [who] eats away the substance of the honeybees' hard work.

Lyric Poems and Historical Writing

Other types of verses the Greeks produced and enjoyed were much shorter and less complex than the epics. Many fell into the category of lyric poems, so named because they were initially meant to be recited or sung while someone played a small harp called a lyre. For themes, they drew mainly on everyday life experiences and common human feelings and emotions. While epic poems were formal and larger-than-life, lyric poems were mostly informal and realistic.

One of the more popular early Greek lyric poets, Archilochus, was born on the Aegean island of Paros in the seventh century BCE. A witty individual, he was at his best when poking fun at people, traditional customs, and even himself. In a poem titled "My Kind of General," he said, "I don't like a general who towers over the troops, lordly with elegant locks and trim [mustache]. Give me a stumpy soldier glaringly bowlegged, yet rock-firm on his feet, and in his heart a giant." Another inventive lyric poet, Xenophanes, penned this brief ditty about religious belief: "If a horse or lion or a slow ox had agile hands for paint and sculpture, the horse would make his god a horse, [and] the ox would sculpt an ox."

Not all lyric poems were meant to be clever or humorous. Many dealt with love, death, and other themes in more serious ways. Some of the most beautiful examples were composed by the female poet Sappho, known for her simple, gentle expressions of friendship and love. "Some might say," she wrote, that "I will love [you] as long as there is breath in me. I'll care. [And] things [might become] grievous [or] bitter, but know that [even then] I will love [you]."

Although the Greeks greatly enjoyed such creative explorations of current feelings and customs, they were also fascinated by past events. Moreover, some of them felt compelled to record the events of their own time for the benefit of future generations. This was why they invented the literary genre of historical writing. The first known conventional history book was the *Histories* of Herodotus. He set out to chronicle the two invasions of Greece by the Persians between 490 and 479 BCE. But in so doing he also provided detailed coverage of the customs and beliefs of many of the peoples the Persians had already conquered. To learn about these things firsthand, he traveled widely through Egypt and the Middle East.

One drawback of Herodotus's book was his inclusion of some hearsay and tall tales he encountered in his travels. The first historian to stick only to verifiable facts was his younger contemporary, the Athenian Thucydides. The latter produced a detailed account of the bloody Peloponnesian War, which began in 431 BCE. He decided to approach the work as a documentary of the conflict as it unfolded and vowed

A statue of Herodotus outside of the Austrian
Parliament Building in Vienna

to include only eyewitness events. In the book's opening, he
wrote, "Either I was present myself at the events which I have
described or else I heard of them from eye-witnesses whose
reports I have checked." The results were impressive to say
the least. The modern military historian Donald Kagan called
Thucydides's book "a masterpiece of historical writing" and
"a foundation stone of historical method."

Speech-Writing

Another formal kind of literature at which the Greeks excelled was speech-writing, sometimes called oratory. Anyone who wanted to impart information directly to others had to either write a letter or stand before them and deliver a speech. Many speeches were political, like the ones given by citizens in Athens's Assembly.

Modern experts generally agree that the most gifted Greek political orator was the Athenian Demosthenes, and that his finest orations were his *Philippics* and *Olynthiacs*. They denounced the Macedonian ruler, Philip II, and warned the Athenians and other Greeks that Philip planned to conquer them all. In his *First Philippic* Demosthenes thundered:

> Observe, Athenians, the height to which the fellow's insolence has soared. [He] cannot rest content with what he has conquered. He is always taking in more, everywhere casting his net round us, while we sit idle and do nothing. When, Athenians, will you take the necessary action? What are you waiting for? Until you are compelled, I presume.

Another form of ancient oratory consisted of court speeches, composed by trained individuals called *logographai*. There were no professional lawyers. And people who needed either to prosecute someone or to defend themselves against a legal charge often did not know how to prepare an effective presentation to the jury. So they hired such speech-writers. Of the few surviving examples of these documents, among the best are those of the Athenians Antiphon and Lysias. In 403 BCE Lysias wrote a speech for a murder case that he prosecuted himself. At one point he told the jury:

I, members of the jury, a man who has never before engaged in litigation . . . am now driven by events to bring this charge against the defendant. [I fear] that my inexperience may cause me to conduct my accusation in an unskilled manner. [But] I shall try to put the facts before you from the beginning, in the fewest possible words, as best I can.

Lysias was a speech writer in Ancient Greece. He was one of the ten Attic orators.

The Novel

In Lysias's day, most people became familiar with such speeches only when they were present in court and heard them firsthand. This was because a majority of people, including many Greeks, could not read. That situation changed markedly, however, in the Hellenistic Age. Lasting from 323 to 30 BCE, when large Greek kingdoms stretched across the Middle East, it witnessed expanded educational opportunities. And for the first time in history, a substantial reading public developed.

To meet the rising demand for reading materials, writers started turning out a wide range of literature. Some was of high quality and aimed at well-educated people. Quite a bit more was aimed at the masses of readers of average ability.

Unacquainted with Love

A few ancient Greek novels were of higher quality than most. One of the best was *Daphnis and Chloe*, by Longus, written in the third century CE when Greece was under Roman rule. In this passage, the young woman Chloe has fallen in love with a fellow shepherd, Daphnis. But she is unaware that what she feels is love:

She did not know what was wrong with her, for she was only a young girl who had been brought up in the country and had never even heard the word "love" used by anyone else. But she felt sick at heart, and she could not control her eyes, and she was always talking about Daphnis.

Members of the latter group read mainly prose fiction in a new literary form—the novel. Greek novels nearly always had a pair of young lovers as the main characters. Typically, a series of misfortunes caused the lovers to be separated for a while, causing worry or suffering, but most commonly they were reunited in the end.

Most of the thousands of ancient Greek novels are gone forever. And the same can be said for the huge output of other Greek literary genres. As the late historian Will Durant put it, "All in all, not more than one-twentieth survives from the critically acclaimed literature of fifth-century BCE Greece, and from the earlier and later centuries even less." Even so, the little that *has* survived has helped to shape Western ideas and literature in profound ways. Those remnants make up "the well-spring of Western letters," historian W. G. Hardy wrote. "In its clarity of thought, perfection of form, directness, and humanism, Greek literature [is] an eternal achievement of the mind and spirit."

Chapter Six:
Monumental Architecture

One early modern visitor to Athens was so moved by what he saw there that he declared, "All the world's culture culminated in Greece, all Greece in Athens, all Athens in its Acropolis, all the Acropolis in the Parthenon." As time went on, this often-cited opinion came to be shared by untold numbers of architects, historians, and ordinary observers alike.

Today, the Parthenon, a large temple built to honor Athens's patron deity, Athena, goddess of wisdom and war, lies in an advanced state of ruin. Yet when people gaze on it, they can instinctively sense they are seeing the remnants of something truly magnificent. An English traveler who saw it in 1809 declared, "The portion of the Parthenon yet standing, cannot fail to fill the mind of the most indifferent spectator with sentiments of astonishment and awe." That sight similarly affected historian John A. Crow when he climbed to the Acropolis's summit in 1970. He later remarked that every person deserved to see the ruined Parthenon at least once before he or she died.

Erected during Athens's cultural golden age in the 400s BCE, the Parthenon is indeed likely the pinnacle of ancient Greek architecture. Nevertheless, the Greeks produced

A modern illustration of ancient Athens and the Acropolis

hundreds of other temples in the same style. They also created numerous other examples of monumental stone architecture, including palaces, fortresses, theaters, public altars, and tombs for royalty. The legacy of these edifices is not simply that their ruins are impressive and emotionally moving. Greek architecture also made a profound impression on later peoples, who copied, and continue to copy, its styles.

Bronze Age Palaces and Fortresses

The palaces and fortresses mentioned above were ancient Greece's first monumental stone structures. They were erected during the Bronze Age (ca. 3000-ca. 1100 BCE), when people used tools and weapons made of bronze, an alloy of copper and tin. The Minoans, centered on the large Greek island of Crete, were at the time Europe's most culturally advanced people. They constructed a number of sprawling "palace-centers." Archaeologists most often use that term rather than "palaces" because they were administrative and food-distribution centers as well as royal residences.

The largest and most imposing of these structures was the one at Knossos, situated about three miles (five kilometers) from Crete's northern coast. Modern excavations have shown that it was constructed on multiple levels and was amazingly complex and sophisticated. David Sacks provided a general description:

> Built mainly of large blocks of Cretan limestone, the palace survives today mostly as a network of foundations and wall remnants covering five and a half acres. Around a central, square courtyard measuring 82 by 180 feet, the building contained pillared hallways, staircases, and hundreds of rooms and storage chambers in a maze-like configuration. There were two or even three upper floors, now partly reconstructed. Among the palace's splendors was running water carried by clay pipes.

Sacks is only one of many modern observers to call the Knossos palace-center "maze-like." This is significant because some now think the building was the inspiration for the mythical Labyrinth, the maze in which the hero Theseus slew the Minotaur, a monster half-bull and half-human.

On the Greek mainland, meanwhile, dwelled another people, the Mycenaeans, who were strongly influenced by Minoan culture. The Mycenaeans also raised monumental buildings in which their rulers lived. These were considerably more fortified than their Minoan counterparts, which had no defensive walls. In contrast, the mainland palaces were surrounded by walls made of gigantic, irregular boulders, some of which measured ten-to-twenty feet across. The Mycenaean palaces themselves were composed of large stones that fitted together with remarkable precision. These structures were as impressive in ruin as they were when in use. After they were abandoned at the close of the Bronze Age, later generations of Greeks thought they had been built by a race of giants.

A Mycenaean Megaron

The inside of a Mycenaean fortress revolved around a broad central hall called a megaron. Archaeologist William R. Biers explains that such a chamber was

> a free-standing unit composed of a more or less square room entered at one side through a porch with two columns and sometimes an anteroom with the same width as the main room. The principal room was dominated by a round fixed hearth, and a platform for a throne was situated against the wall opposite it. The hearth was supported by four columns, which held up the roof. Megara were two stories high, and [had] a smoke opening [with] chimney pipes to draw off the smoke.

Temples: From Wood to Stone

During Greece's Dark Age (ca. 1100-ca. 800 BCE), which followed the collapse of its Bronze-Age civilization, the inhabitants were impoverished, illiterate, and created no monumental architecture. However, by the end of the first century of the Archaic Age (ca. 800-ca. 500 BCE) prosperity had returned. Greece was now composed of hundreds of small city-states, which viewed themselves as separate nations. Yet they shared the same pantheon of gods, which they devotedly worshiped. So each state had one or more religious temples.

As a rule, the main temple in a city was dedicated to the local divine patron, a god thought to give that community special attention and protection. The Greeks believed that said deity actually visited the temple from time to time. So to respect the god's privacy, no worship took place inside the building, as it does in modern churches. Instead, altars for conducting sacrifices to the god were erected outside, either on the temple steps or elsewhere on the grounds. (The temple and its sacred grounds were together called a sanctuary.)

The earliest temples were rectangular, of modest size, and made of wood and other perishable materials. Over time, they rapidly grew in size. And each came to be encased by colonnades, or rows of columns, running along each of the structure's four sides. This feature became standard in temple architecture. So did front and back porches, each fronted by a broad staircase; and a low-pitched roof forming a pediment, or triangular space, above the colonnade on each end.

The builders increasingly desired to place statues and other decorative elements inside the pediments, along the roof perimeter, and elsewhere on such structures. They also began replacing the thatched roofs with pottery roofing tiles. Both the decorative elements and tiles were very heavy, and it quickly became clear that wooden columns and walls were not strong enough to bear the load. So in the mid-600s BCE builders began switching to stone. Within about a century, all-stone temples had become the rule across the Greek lands.

Temples: Proportions and Orders

Whether made of stone or wood, Greek temples were not just large-scale structures made to house and show respect for the gods. As they evolved, they also became physical, tangible expressions of the builders' intellects and emotions. The century in which stone temples were rising across Greece was the same one in which Greek scientists were searching for simple, practical, logical explanations for what makes the universe tick. And the rational spirit that drove that journey of discovery infused other Greek creative endeavors, including architecture. The late scholar of ancient Greece, Edith Hamilton wrote:

> The Greek temple is the perfect expression
> of the pure intellect illumined by the spirit.

No other great building anywhere approaches its simplicity. [It] is the home of humanity at ease, calm, ordered, sure of itself and the world. [It is] majestic but human. . . . To the Greek architect, man was master of the world. His mind could understand its laws. His spirit could discover its beauty.

Searching for just the right sense of balance and proportions in constructing temples, Greek architects experimented with different ratios of length to width. And over time they arrived at a consensus. They agreed that the most eye-pleasing ratio was two-to-one. As a result, most of their temples built from the mid-sixth century BCE on had six columns on each end and thirteen columns on each side.

They also settled on two basic architectural orders, or styles—the Doric and Ionic. A third order, the Corinthian, was added about two centuries later. Art historian Thomas Craven offered a simple description of these orders, which were based on the distinctive design of the capitals, or tops, of their columns: "There is the Doric column with the simple, expanding cushion for the capital; the Ionic, with the double scroll, or volutes, at the top; and the Corinthian, distinguished by its sprouting of chicory leaves at the upper end of the [column's] shaft."

Column styles from top to bottom: Doric, Ionic, and Corinthian

Temple-Building on the Acropolis

One of the finest of the all-stone Doric temples raised in Greece in the late 500s BCE was the Temple of Athena Polias (Athena "of the City"). It stood atop the Athenian Acropolis, allowing it to be seen for miles in all directions. The exact details of the structure are uncertain because the Persians wrecked it when they invaded Greece in 480 BCE.

After the intruders were driven out, the Athenians decided to leave the ruins as they were as a memorial to the victory. But that policy changed a generation later. In the 440s BCE, the popular general Pericles spearheaded an exceptionally ambitious building program. He advocated clearing the ruins on the Acropolis and erecting a huge new complex of temples and statues of gods there. The project ended up producing three temples, all dedicated to Athena, including the Temple of Athena Nike (Athena "the Victor") and the Erechtheum. It was the third one—the Parthenon—that became the most famous of all ancient Greek structures.

Like the building it replaced, the Parthenon was Doric in style. It was conceived on a much grander scale, however. It retained the two-to-one ratio of length to width, but instead of six columns across the front and thirteen along the side, it had an eight-by-seventeen arrangement. All of the structure's other features were necessarily larger as a result. In its finished form, it was 65 feet (20m) high, 237 feet (72m) long, and 110 feet (33m) wide. The building was impressive not only for its size, but also for its artistic effects. In addition to its numerous superb sculptures of people and animals, like other Greek temples it was painted in bright colors, especially red and blue. (Later, the corrosive effects of many centuries of weathering steadily erased those pigments.)

The colossal statue of Athena that stood inside the temple's cella, or main room, was also partially painted. Towering to nearly 40 feet (12m), this magnificent creation was made of wood, ivory, and roughly 2,500 pounds (1,135kg) of pure gold. It was crafted by Pericles's friend, Phidias, who later came to be seen as the ancient world's greatest sculptor.

A Form of Propaganda

The tremendous time, labor, and expense required to assemble the Parthenon were not expended simply out of religious devotion. Such large-scale building projects were also a form of propaganda. Pericles and his supporters wanted to impress rival Greek states and to trumpet Athens's importance to the world.

"You should fix your eyes every day on the greatness of Athens," he proclaimed, "and should fall in love with her. When you realize her greatness, then reflect that what made her great was men with a spirit of adventure." Also, historian Thomas Martin points out, the Parthenon's splendor suggested there was "a special intimacy between the city-state and the gods." The temple therefore "expressed the Athenian view that the gods looked favorably on their empire."

Other Public Buildings

The standard architectural style used for temples was so popular in Greece that it came to be employed in other types of public buildings. Among them were treasuries. Looking like miniature temples, treasuries were highly decorated structures in which communities kept gold and other valuables. Another common structure that looked like a small temple was a fountain house. It was most commonly constructed beside a stream to allow water to flow inside, where it was stored. People who lived nearby brought buckets and filled them by turning on a small faucet projecting from the building's outer wall.

Temples, treasuries, and fountain houses remained common public buildings in Greece throughout the Classical Age (ca. 500-323 BCE). The period that followed—the Hellenistic Age (323-30 BCE)—witnessed the appearance of a new and visually striking form of architecture, the monumental step-altar. Outdoor altars had been used since the Dark Age, but they were typically small—about the size of a large brick barbecue. In comparison, the Hellenistic altars were incorporated into massive stone platforms fronted by huge staircases. They were also decorated with statues, colonnades, and ornate bands of sculptures. The largest and most beautiful was the Great Altar of Zeus, in the Greek kingdom of Pergamum, in northwestern Anatolia.

The general look of these altars influenced architects in later ages. The Piazza del Campidoglio, in Rome, designed by the Renaissance master Michelangelo, is an example. Reached by an enormous staircase, the Cordonata, the Piazza is a splendid oval-shaped plaza decorated by large statues. Another modern example is the front facade of the U.S. Library of Congress, in Washington, D.C. In designing its staircases and colonnades, the architects consciously imitated the Pergamum altar.

The Court of Neptune Fountain in front of the Library of Congress's Jefferson Building

Also in Washington is the U.S. Supreme Court Building, designed to look like a Roman version of a Greek temple. Indeed, the Romans borrowed Greek temple architecture and passed it along to the modern world, where thousands of courthouses, government buildings, and banks still utilize it. The fact that Greek architectural styles are still so widely admired and copied would not have surprised Pericles. Standing before his countrymen, in sight of the awe-inspiring Parthenon, he correctly predicted, "Future ages will wonder at us, as the present age wonders at us now."

Chapter Seven:
Athletic Games and Sports

When the first modern Olympic Games were held in Athens in 1896, they were far from a new idea. The games were a revival of the ancient Olympics, named for the site where they were held for nearly twelve centuries—Olympia, in southwestern Greece. These contests were one of the handful of cultural traditions, including language and religious beliefs, that brought together the otherwise fiercely independent and disunited Greek states.

These intense feelings of independence were largely the source of the ingrained spirit of competition that inspired and maintained the Olympics and other athletic games in Greece. Deep within the Greek psyche was a powerful yearning or need to achieve great things and to be the best at doing it. According to David C. Young, professor of classics at the University of Florida:

> In that quest for distinction through excellence, we find the driving force behind Greek athletics, [and] in the readiness of adult men to run the naked risk of public dishonor [by losing] for the chance to achieve distinction, there we find what separated the Greeks out from other peoples.

It should be emphasized that the Greeks did not psycho-analyze themselves. That is, they did not sit around trying to figure out why they were so drawn to what they called the *agon*, translating as both a contest and a struggle. (They also used the term to describe lawsuits and battles.) They simply loved sports—to play them and to compete in them for prizes or glory. And they did both on a grand scale. The late educator, writer, and historian Edith Hamilton wrote:

> All over Greece there were games, athletic contests of every description [and] games so many that one grows weary with the list of them. . . . If we had no other knowledge of what the Greeks were like, [the] fact that they were in love with play and played magnificently would be proof enough of how they [viewed] life.

The Mind-body Ideal

It is unclear exactly when this passionate love of athletics rooted itself in Greek society and thought. But it is fairly certain that by the early years of the Archaic Age many Greeks, particularly young men, played sports, not only in formal contests, but also in backyard settings. So physical fitness was a must.

To this end, from early in life boys were immersed in a pervasive physical culture, consisting of a wide range of social institutions and customs revolving around fitness and athletic training. For boys there were wrestling schools in every town. Wrestling was the most popular sport and appealed to the Greeks in the same way that baseball and football and basketball do to Americans. And young men worked out in local gymnasia, which were as common then as grocery stores are today.

As physical fitness, sports, and excelling in both became second nature to most Greek males (and in a few places females), a new mental attitude emerged. It was called *kalokagathia*, essentially meaning the "mind-body ideal." In applying it to life, one tried to excel in physical, intellectual, and moral endeavors with the goal of becoming as rounded and admirable as possible.

Initially, this ambitious personal objective was popular mainly among members of the upper classes and seen as out of the reach of "ordinary" folk. However, with the spread of democracy in the fifth and fourth centuries BCE, some men in all social classes strove for the mind-body ideal. (The word *ideal* must be stressed here. Not every person had the physical and mental gifts needed to excel in all things. Nor was every Greek motivated to do so.)

The Olympic Truce and the Altis

Whether or not a Greek athlete strove to be an ideal person, he and his opponents agreed that taking part in the games was not simply a form of play. It had a serious dimension, too, because these contests were staged to honor the gods. The Olympics and other leading competitions were held on lands seen as sacred and comprised one element among several in a yearly religious festival. Those who competed understood that the physical skills they displayed and any victories they might win were meant to gratify and honor one or more gods.

Of these major athletic games, four that attracted contestants from across the Greek world had emerged by the end of the sixth century BCE. The Olympics, dedicated to Zeus, was the most prestigious. It was held every four years, a period that became known as an Olympiad. The other three major competitions were the Nemean Games, also honoring Zeus, staged every two years at Nemea, in south-central Greece; the Pythian Games, devoted to Apollo, held at Delphi in the third year of each Olympiad; and the Isthmian Games, dedicated to Poseidon, god of the seas, held every two years at Corinth. Those four large-scale competitions were together called the *periodos*, or "circuit."

The summit of the circuit, the Olympics, took place in Olympia's sacred sanctuary, the Altis. Because the site was situated on lands belonging to the city-state of Elis, the Eleans served as hosts of the games, a very prestigious duty. One responsibility of the Elean government was to send out three heralds, the "Truce-Bearers," shortly before the start of each Olympiad. These officials traveled to every Greek state and announced the exact date of the coming games. They also proclaimed the Olympic truce. Originally it lasted for a month, but later it was extended to three. Judith Swaddling, assistant keeper in the Department of Greek and Roman Antiquities at the British Museum and author of *The Ancient Olympic Games*, explains:

> The terms of the truce were engraved on a bronze discus which was kept in the Temple of Hera in the Altis. It forbade states participating in the games to take up arms, to pursue legal disputes, or to carry out death penalties. This was to ensure that pilgrims and athletes traveling to and from Olympia would have a safe journey. Violators of the truce were heavily fined.

The Olympic Judges

In the earliest Olympiads, in the 700s BCE, the principal elders of the Elean community selected two judges to supervise the athletic events. Over the years, however, the games attracted increasing numbers of athletes and spectators, which necessitated more judges. So by the early 400s BCE there were ten, now picked from among the Elean citizens through random drawing. The judges, who wore impressive purple robes, had the authority to punish rule breakers, at times severely. For instance, a competitor who took a bribe might be publicly whipped.

In the weeks preceding the games, people from far and wide began to converge on Olympia. There they found a large cluster of buildings and facilities, including temples honoring Zeus, his divine wife Hera, and his mother Rhea. Near Rhea's temple was a long row of treasuries in which visitors placed valuables intended as offerings to the gods. Surrounding the temples were athletic venues, among them a hippodrome (outdoor racetrack) for horse and chariot races, a stadium for track and field events, a large gymnasium, and a wrestling facility.

Olympia, Greece, as depicted in a hand-colored
nineteenth-century illustration

The Olympic Program

The masses of spectators, athletes, and assorted others had no sooner gotten settled when the games began. They took place over the course of five days. The first day consisted of ceremonial and religious events. The athletes swore an oath to Zeus that they would compete honestly and the judges swore they would be fair and not take any bribes. The oaths were followed by prayers, public sacrifices, and speeches by various dignitaries and scholars.

The second day of the Olympic program witnessed the beginning of the athletic events. The horse and chariot races were held in the hippodrome in the morning and the pentathlon took place in the stadium in the afternoon. The pentathlon combined five track and field events—running, jumping, the discus throw, the javelin throw, and wrestling. In the evening, there were feasts for the athletes.

Putting Up with Discomforts

Watching the ancient Olympics was often uncomfortable, partly because of the enormous crowds. Also, the games took place in August, when temperatures reached almost 90 degrees. The first-century Greek thinker Epictetus wrote about his visits to Olympia and why it was worth it to put up with the discomforts:

Aren't you scorched there by the fierce heat? Aren't you crushed in the crowd? Isn't it difficult to freshen yourself up? Doesn't the rain soak you to the skin? Aren't you bothered by the noise [and] other nuisances? But it seems to me that you are well able to bear and indeed gladly endure all this, when you think of the gripping spectacles that you will see.

On the third day, the athletes and officials marched in a dignified manner to Zeus's outdoor altar, not far from that god's temple. There, priests sacrificed a hundred oxen to him. Then a series of contests for boys between the ages of twelve and eighteen were held.

The next day, the fourth in the program, was devoted to the adult footraces and combat events—boxing, wrestling, and the pankration. The latter was a very rough mixture of wrestling and boxing similar to modern mixed martial arts, or "ultimate fighting." It was not uncommon for pankrationists to suffer serious injuries or even die during their matches.

Finally came the fifth and last day of the Olympics. First came a stately ceremony in which the victors were crowned with laurel leaves. Then more feasts, sacrifices, and festivities were held.

The Athenian Games

Athletes and spectators who attended the games at Delphi, Nemea, and Isthmia found programs of events, athletic facilities, and crowds similar to those at Olympia, though on a somewhat lesser scale. In addition, numerous smaller competitions were staged for religious festivals in individual city-states. Because Athens was the richest Greek state, it is not surprising that it had the biggest and most popular local games. They were part of the city's chief festival—the Panathenaea, staged annually, but celebrated on a larger scale every fourth year.

Athletes in the Panathenaea competed in two separate programs of events, one featuring chariot races and others that appeared in the programs of the circuit games. These were usually open to both Athenians and Greeks from other cities. The second program included events open only to Athenian citizens, among them several that were not offered in the Olympics and other circuit games. One was a parade in which two-horse chariots took part. Modern scholars believe the judges scored the participants on their ability to march and drill as precisely as possible.

Other events open only to Athenians were the tribal competitions. (As was the case with other Greek states, Athens had several traditional tribes, each composed of a number of families related by blood.) An especially popular tribal contest was a torch-race for teams of men. (There was also a torch race for individual competitors.) The teams were large, having up to forty runners. Each man sprinted roughly two hundred feet, then passed a burning torch to a teammate, who then ran the same distance and passed the torch on, and so forth. This relay race went on for a mile and a half. In his famous work, the *Republic*, the Athenian scholar Plato mentioned a variation of the event in which the torch-carriers rode horses.

The Myth of Amateurism

Whether they were large-scale, like the Olympics, or smaller, like those in local cities, Greek athletic contests happened very long ago. And some of the evidence for the events, rules, and customs was lost over the centuries. So modern scholars continue to debate certain aspects of these games.

One such argument was finally settled in the late twentieth century. For a long time a majority of historians held that the only prize victorious ancient athletes received was the crown of laurel leaves presented at Olympia and other circuit games. In this view, that award was enough for the competitors because they were motivated primarily from their love of sport. They were "gentleman amateurs," the argument went. As a result of this supposition, the early organizers of the modern Olympics prohibited participation by professional, or paid, athletes.

This theory proved to be wrong, however. Evidence eventually showed that the modern notion of amateur athletics was alien to the Greeks. Although victors at the Olympics did receive laurel crowns, the athletes also enjoyed generous financial backing from well-to-do citizens in their home cities. Also, when they returned home the winners received awards

A 1922 lithograph of runners competing in the Athenian relay race

such as expensive jars of olive oil and bronze tripods, which they could sell for a profit. It was not unusual for a victorious runner to get the equivalent of two or more years' salary for winning a single race.

Some people feel that knowing Greek athletes obtained material rewards for their efforts somehow tarnishes their image. Others look to the bloated salaries of today's professional sports stars and point out that nothing has really changed in that regard.

Also unchanged are many of the ancient track and field events. They remain alive in the modern Olympics, which itself was directly borrowed from the Greeks. And practically every high school and college in the world has a track and field team on which an ancient Greek sprinter or discus thrower would feel perfectly at home.

Chapter Eight:
Enduring Military Traditions

Today, it is taken for granted in Western democracies like the United States and Britain that national armies are made up of citizens who elect the governments that declare and run any wars that arise. This idea was introduced by the Greeks some twenty-five centuries ago. Before the Greeks, and after them in many parts of the world, large portions of the armies fielded by kings, emperors, and other absolute monarchs were made up of reluctant soldiers. Most had no say in choosing their rulers. And they had no desire to risk their lives for the personal whims or poor judgment of those leaders. Yet when the dictator commanded it, they had no choice but to fight. It is no wonder that their performance on the battlefield was often mediocre.

In marked contrast, most Greek citizen-soldiers had at least some say in choosing both their leaders and whether to go to war. And that made them more willing to train for the contingency of war and more eager to defend their countries when an enemy threatened. Moreover, their singular attitude toward military service endured in Europe and in the fullness of time became the mantra of modern Western armies. Military historian Victor Davis Hanson wrote:

> Western armies [are] subject to civilian control
> and audit. Their soldiers, like Greek [fighters] of
> old, are not shanghaied [forced] into service, but
> enter the armed forces with understood rights
> and responsibilities. . . . In short, western mili-
> tary forces are composed of better-trained and
> disciplined troops, which are better equipped
> and led by better generals than any others in the
> world today. . . . What makes Western arms so
> accomplished [is] a series of practices created at
> the beginning of Western culture by the Greeks.

These practices include the creation of a citizenry willing
to fight to defend shared culture and ideals; an emphasis on
the physical strength and enthusiasm of infantry (foot soldiers);
superior organization and discipline; and an effort to craft the
most effective weapons using the best available materials and
newest technologies.

Hoplites and Their Panoply

The creation of these early Western military practices went
hand-in-hand with the rise of the Greek city-states between
about 800 and 600 BCE. Just as farmers and shopkeepers
became the supportive forces of the economies and political assemblies of these states, they also manned their armies.
Initially, the farmers needed to protect their lands from the
farmers of neighboring states. So they organized citizen mili-
tias to settle border disputes in what were usually brief but
bloody battles.

In this way the city-states developed small but effective
armies of part-time soldiers to defend both land and other
national interests. These soldiers were infantrymen known
as hoplites, probably after the word *hopla*, meaning "heavy
equipment." That equipment consisted of bronze armor and
the thrusting spears and short swords with which they fought.
As Hanson points out:

Hoplite warfare [made] perfect sense. Muster the largest, best-armed group of farmers to protect land in the quickest, cheapest, and most decisive way possible. It was far easier and more economical for farmers to defend farmland than to tax and hire landless others. [Warfare] was now a civic matter, an issue to be voted on by free landowning infantrymen themselves. As such, hoplite fighting . . . marks the true beginning of Western warfare.

The considerable weight of a hoplite's armor and weapons led to the term "heavy infantry," which was widely used in the West thereafter.

Together, his arms and armor made up his panoply. The most basic element of the panoply was the shield, in Greek the *hoplon*, on average three feet across and weighing about seventeen pounds. Typically the shield was composed of a wooden core reinforced on the outside by a coating of bronze or several layers of ox-hide.

A modern illustration of a heavily armed Greek hoplite

Hoplite Shield Devices

Hoplites traditionally decorated the outer surfaces of their shields with emblems or designs collectively called shield "devices." Some, including the faces of mythical monsters, were intended to rattle an enemy's nerves. Others designated military rank or family background. And in many cases the device was a letter of the alphabet, usually the first letter in the name of the soldier's home state. Spartan hoplites, for instance, put an L on their shields. It stood for Lakedaimon, Sparta's traditional ancient name. Similarly, hoplites from Athens used an A; those from Messenia an M; Sicyonia an S; and Tegea a T. Pictures of objects were also popular. For example, the shield device of soldiers from Mantinea was a trident (three-pronged spear), the symbol of their patron god, Poseidon.

Among the other elements of the hoplite's panoply was his cuirass, a breastplate or torso-protector. The most expensive kind was made of bronze and had sculpted chest and abdominal muscles in the front. Much more common were cuirasses composed of several layers of linen or canvas glued together to make a rigid shirt. Complementing the cuirass were: a bronze helmet, sometimes topped by decorative horse-hair plumes; bronze shin-guards called greaves; the hoplite's principal weapon—a seven-foot-long thrusting spear; and an iron sword used mainly as a back-up weapon if his spear broke.

The Greek Phalanx

Once the hoplites had donned their panoplies, they formed ranks in their principal battlefield formation. Called a phalanx, it was a long block of soldiers standing in ranks, or lines, one behind another. Eight ranks was the average depth, but when a general deemed it necessary it could be as few as three or four or more than eight.

The exact organization of most Greek phalanxes is unclear. In some cases this was because the military leaders of the city-states kept that sort of information secret to maintain an edge over enemies. By far, more details are known about Athens's phalanx (and its military customs in general) than those of its rivals. Evidence shows that the Athenian phalanx had ten subdivisions, each with a commander who reported to the strategos in charge of the army. And each of the ten subdivisions was composed of several smaller units, probably having a hundred men each.

Most scholars think that this general breakdown was fairly typical of most Greek phalanxes in the Classical period. The size of Athens's version was larger than most others. This was because Athens was Greece's wealthiest and most populous city and could afford to assemble bigger armies. Often Athens fielded as many as 10,000 hoplites or even more. This dwarfed most other city-state armies, which likely consisted of from five hundred to 2,000 men each.

The phalanx of Athens's arch-rival, Sparta, most commonly had between 2,000 and 3,000 hoplites during the Classical Age. But though this was less than a third the size of Athens's army, the Spartans actually had the advantage over the Athenians in most land battles. This was because Sparta had an extremely rigid and efficient system for training its soldiers. Called the *agoge* (uh-GO-gee), it took seven-year-old boys from their homes, placed them in military barracks for two decades or more, and turned them into virtual killing machines. The Spartan phalanx was so formidable and feared that it was long viewed as invincible. (It was finally defeated by the Thebans in a pivotal battle in 371 BCE.)

Greek Against Greek

The reputations of the individual combatants aside, when two Greek phalanxes prepared to clash, they followed highly formal warfare rituals. Often the leaders notified each other of their intent to fight, and the two armies met in a predetermined place. Then they marched at each other and smashed together.

Fortunately for the men in each phalanx, their formation gave them a great deal of protection. In battle mode they stood about two to three feet apart and held their shields up, creating an unbroken barrier hundreds or in some cases thousands of feet wide. "Every shield protected not only its user's left side," military historian John Warry writes, "but also the right side and [spear] arm of his neighbor."

With both sides nearly equally protected by armor, victory was often determined by the sheer stamina, or lack thereof, of the participants. This was because a Greek phalanx possessed seemingly unstoppable forward momentum. As the men in its front rank made contact with the enemy front line, their companions in the rear ranks pushed at their backs, driving them forward with tremendous force. This pushing action was called the *othismos*, or "the shoving." So battles between opposing phalanxes frequently turned into giant shoving matches in which the two armies pushed each other back and forth until one side gave way. When one side did begin to collapse, its members most commonly retreated.

The chief reason this peculiar form of warfare developed among the Greek states appears to be that it minimized the killing of civilians and destruction of towns on both sides. With occasional exceptions, a war consisted of a single brief and decisive battle fought away from populated areas. This "left the property and culture of the defeated intact," Hanson explained. "Hoplite conflict was by deliberate design . . . intended to focus a concentrated brutality upon a few in order to spare the many."

Also, because of the excellent protection provided by the hoplites' panoplies, relatively few of them died in a typical battle. Military historians estimate that at most 10 to 15 percent were killed. In this way, prolonged, ruinous wars were rare during the Classical Age. (The principal exception was the Peloponnesian War, fought on and off from 431 to 404 BCE.)

Greek Against Non-Greek

Things were very different when Greeks fought non-Greeks. A typical Greek army of that era could easily defeat a non-Greek army two or three times its size. This was proven time and again as armies of Greek hoplites demolished much larger ones fielded by foreign enemies. The most notable example was the Persian Empire, then the biggest empire in the world.

Among the reasons for this remarkable string of victories were that the Greeks were better-armored, better-trained, and better-disciplined. Also, the Persians and others whom the Greeks fought in Classical times did not use the phalanx and could not stand up to its extraordinary offensive power. Many of those who tried were slaughtered. The second-century BCE Greek historian Polybius did not exaggerate when he said, "So long as the phalanx retains its characteristic form and strength, nothing can withstand its charge or resist it face to face."

They Turned and Fled

Non-Greeks who saw the formidable shield-wall of a Greek phalanx approaching were often terrified. And on occasion they simply turned and ran for their lives. The Greek adventurer and historian Xenophon (ZEN-uh-fon) described the reaction of a Persian army to a Greek one of which he himself was a member:

> The two lines were hardly six or seven hundred yards apart when [we] began to chant the battle hymn and then charged [the Persians] at the double. [But suddenly they] turned and fled. At once [we] pursued [them] with might and main. . . . No Greeks were hurt in this battle, except one on the left wing, said to have been shot by an arrow.

Soldiers of the Macedonian phalanx, as illustrated in the
1908 book *Harmsworth History of the World*

The Greeks' reputation for military prowess continued after the Classical Age. Late in that period, they developed an even more lethal kind of phalanx, which continued to be used during Hellenistic times. Called the Macedonian phalanx because it was perfected by Macedonia's King Philip II, father of Alexander the Great, it had deeper ranks than earlier versions. Also, Philip armed its members with long battle pikes called *sarissas*. Thousands of them protruded from the formation's front, giving it the look of a giant porcupine with its quills erect.

The Hellenistic Greeks also developed new kinds of military technology. Among them were mechanical killing machines, including catapults and rock- and spear-throwers (the first examples of artillery); all manner of siege machines, some of which were so enormous they could hold hundreds of men; and battle elephants that carried archers and javelin-throwers on their backs.

Yet all of these advances were secondary to the Greeks' first and primary military invention. It was the pitched battle fought by infantrymen trying to quickly and decisively devastate the enemy while incurring minimal casualties on their own side. This calculated and often lethal military tradition passed from Greece to Rome. And the Romans, who were masters of using other peoples' ideas to their own advantage, improved on it so well that they eventually conquered the Greeks.

In another unexpected turn of events, after Rome's government fell the Romanized version of the Greek way of war did not disappear with it. In the centuries that followed, the Greco-Roman military legacy lay dormant for a while, was rediscovered during the Renaissance, and went on to help the modern West capture large sectors of the globe. The Greek citizen-farmers who invented hoplite warfare could never have imagined the long and far-reaching series of events they had set in motion.

Timeline

BCE	
ca. 3000-ca. 1100	Greece's Bronze Age, in which people use tools and weapons made of bronze.
ca. 1400	Mycenaean warlords overthrow another early Aegean people, the Minoans, who have long controlled Crete.
ca. 1250-ca. 1200	The approximate time the Trojan War occurred (if it was a real event).
ca. 1100-ca. 800	Greece's Dark Age, in which poverty and illiteracy are widespread.
ca. 800-ca. 500	Greece's Archaic Age, in which prosperity returns and city-states arise.
776	Traditional date for the first Olympic Games, held at Olympia, in southwestern Greece.
594	In Athens, a statesman named Solon negotiates a political settlement that gives considerable authority to non-aristocrats.
547	The Greek philosopher-scientist Anaximander dies.
534	The Athenians institute a new religious festival that includes dramatic contests.
508	An aristocrat named Cleisthenes and his supporters transform Athens's government into the world's first democracy.
ca. 500-323	Greece's Classical Age, in which Greek arts, architecture, literature, and democratic reforms reach their height.
496	The great Athenian playwright Sophocles is born.
490	The Athenians defeat an army of invading Persians at Marathon.

480-479	The Persian king Xerxes leads a massive invasion of Greece; in a series of epic battles, the Greeks drive the invaders away.
472	The Athenian playwright Aeschylus presents *The Persians*, depicting the recent Persian incursion.
446	The Athenian comic playwright Aristophanes is born.
432	The Parthenon, a temple honoring Athens's patron goddess Athena, is completed atop Athens's Acropolis.
431	Sparta declares war on Athens, initiating the disastrous Peloponnesian War.
ca. 429	Sophocles stages his masterpiece, *Oedipus the King*.
ca. 427-347	The lifespan of the Athenian philosopher-scientist Plato.
405	Aristophanes's play *Frogs* premieres.
404	Athens surrenders, ending the Peloponnesian War; the Spartan hegemony of Greece begins.
399	The Athenian philosopher Socrates is tried and executed.
371	Theban leader Epaminondas defeats the Spartans at Leuctra; the Theban hegemony begins.
359	King Philip II takes charge of the culturally backward kingdom of Macedonia and begins forging a formidable army.
338	Philip and his young son Alexander defeat an alliance of city-states at Chaeronea.
336	Philip is assassinated.

✵ Timeline

334	Alexander leads an army into Persia and defeats a Persian force along the Granicus River in Anatolia.
323	After defeating Persia and carving out an enormous empire, Alexander dies in Babylon.
323-30	Greece's Hellenistic Age, in which Greek kingdoms and city-states exist across Greece and the Middle East.
ca. 310	The Greek astronomer Aristarchus, who will propose that earth revolves around the sun, is born.
200	The Romans enter Greece and attack the Macedonian Kingdom.
146	Having defeated most of the Greek states, the Romans destroy the city of Corinth as a warning against further Greek resistance.
31	The Roman leader Octavian defeats the last major independent Greek ruler, Cleopatra VII, at Actium.
30	Cleopatra and her colleague Mark Antony commit suicide, leaving Octavian in control of most of the known world; most modern historians mark this date as the start of the Roman Empire.
27	Octavian is proclaimed Augustus Caesar and is in effect the first Roman emperor.

CE

476	The last western Roman emperor is forced from his throne, marking the end of the western Roman Empire.

❊ Sources

CHAPTER ONE:
A Brief History of Ancient Greece

p. 10,   "High-ranked individuals and families . . ." Sarah B. Pomeroy et al, *Ancient Greece: A Political, Social, and Cultural History* (New York: Oxford University Press, 1999), 8-9.

p. 11,   "These were sophisticated buildings . . ." Charles Freeman, *The Greek Achievement: The Foundation of the Western World* (New York: Viking, 2003), 28.

p. 12,   "the palace-centers were in ruins . . ." Pomeroy et al., *Ancient Greece: A Political, Social, and Cultural History*, 41, 43.

p. 13,   "A significant shift . . ." Thomas R. Martin, *Ancient Greece: From Prehistoric to Hellenistic Times* (New Haven: Yale University Press, 2000), 40.

p. 16,   "Ideas were expressed directly . . ." Chester G. Starr, *The Ancient Greeks* (New York: Oxford University Press, 1981), 49-51.

p. 17,   "Our constitution is called . . ." Thucydides, *The Peloponnesian War*, trans. Richard Crawley (New York: Free Press, 1996), 145.

p. 18,   "the torch to set fire . . ." W. G. Hardy, *The Greek and Roman World* (Westwood, MA: Paperbook Press, 1991), 11.

p. 19,   "The admiration of the present . . ." Thucydides, *The Peloponnesian War*, 114.

p. 22,   "He had great personal beauty . . ." Arrian, *Anabasis Alexandri*, published as *The Campaigns of Alexander*, trans. Aubrey de Sélincourt (New York: Penguin, 1976), 395-396, 398.

p. 26,   "It would be best of all . . ." Polybius, *Histories*, published as *Polybius: The Rise of the Roman Empire*, trans. Ian Scott-Kilvert (New York: Penguin, 1979), 299.

CHAPTER TWO:
Politics and Democracy

p. 29,   "It would be misleading . . ." Pomeroy et al., *Ancient Greece: A Political, Social, and Cultural History*, 47.

p. 30,   "To the people I have given . . ." Kenneth J. Atchity, ed., *The Classical Greek Reader* (New York: Oxford University Press, 1998), 54.

p. 32,   "took the people . . ." Herodotus, *The Histories*, trans. Aubrey de Sélincourt (New York: Penguin, 1996), 364.

p. 32,   "the most democratic form . . ." Michael Grant, *The Rise of the Greeks* (New York: Macmillan, 2005), 69.

p. 34,   "The Council prepared . . ." Lesley Adkins and Roy A. Adkins, *Handbook to Life in Ancient Greece* (New York: Facts On File, 2005), 32.

CHAPTER THREE:
Philosophy and Science

p. 38,   "Warmth lives in moisture . . ." Philip Wheelwright, ed., *The Presocratics* (New York: Macmillan, 1987), 50.

p. 39,   "For how [else] could hair . . ." Ibid, 160-161.

p. 40,   "[When] asked to what end . . ." Laertius, *Lives of the Eminent Philosophers*, Vol. 1, trans. R. D. Hicks (Cambridge, MA: Harvard University Press, 1995), 137, 139, 141.

p. 40,   "the other stars . . ." Diogenes Laertius, *Lives of the Eminent Philosophers*, Vol. 2, 417.

p. 41,   "in order that . . ." Plato, *Timaeus*, in *The Dialogues of Plato*, trans. Benjamin Jowett (Chicago: Encyclopedia Britannica, 1984), 451.

pp. 44-46, "continually carried round . . ." Ibid, 30.

p. 46,   "a series of footnotes . . ." Alfred North Whitehead, *Process and Reality: An Essay in Cosmology*, ed. D. R. Griffin and D. W. Sherburne (New York: Free Press, 1978), 39.

CHAPTER FOUR:
Theaters, Plays, and Acting

p. 48,   "It certainly began . . ." Aristotle, *Poetics*, in *The Complete Works of Aristotle, Vol. 1*, ed., Jonathon Barnes (Princeton: Princeton University Press, 1984), 2319.

p. 49,   "to represent a community . . ." Iris Brooke, *Costume in Greek Classic Drama* (Mineola, NY: Dover, 2003), 77.

p. 50,   "They not only covered . . ." Ibid, 79.

p. 51,   "burst into tears . . ." Herodotus, *Histories*, 395.

p. 52,   "Greek tragedy grew on tales . . ." David Sacks, *Encyclopedia of the Ancient Greek World* (New York: Facts On File, 1995), 241.

p. 53,   "incidents arousing pity . . ." Aristotle, *Poetics*, 2320.

p. 54,   "Many wonders exist . . ." Sophocles, *Antigone*, lines 368-406, trans. Don Nardo.

p. 56,   "was in many ways . . ." Pomeroy, *Ancient Greece: A Political, Social, and Cultural History*, 225.

CHAPTER FIVE:
Poetry and Other Literature

p. 58,   "The most striking quality . . ." C. M. Bowra, *Classical Greece* (New York: Time-Life, 1977), 15.

p. 60,   "their greatest civilizing influence . . ." Grant, *The Rise of the Greeks*, 147.

p. 61,   "Remember what I keep telling you . . ." Hesiod, *Works and Days*, quoted in Atchity, *The Classical Greek Reader*, 33.

pp. 61-62, "I don't like a general . . ." Atchity, *The Classical Greek Reader*, 43.

p. 62,   "If a horse or a lion . . ." Bernard Knox, ed., *The Norton Book of Classical Literature* (New York: Norton, 1993), 233.

p. 62,   "Some might say . . ." Atchity, *The Classical Greek Reader*, 63.

p. 63,   "Either I was present . . ." Thucydides, *The Peloponnesian War*, 48.

p. 63,   "a masterpiece of historical writing . . ." Donald Kagan, *The Peloponnesian War* (New York: Viking, 2003), xxv.

p. 64,   "Observe, Athenians . . ." Demosthenes, *Olynthiacs, Philippics, Minor Speeches*, trans. J. H. Vince (Cambridge, MA: Harvard University Press, 1998), 73-75.

p. 65,   "I, members of the jury . . ." Kathleen Freeman, *The Murder of Herodes and Other Trials from the Athenian Law Courts* (Cambridge, MA: Hackett, 1994), 55.

p. 66,   "She did not know . . ." Atchity, *The Classical Greek Reader*, 357.

p. 66,   "All in all . . ." Will Durant, *The Life of Greece* (New York: MJF, 1997), 436.

p. 66 ,   "the well-spring of Western letters . . ." Hardy, *The Greek and Roman World*, 46.

CHAPTER SIX:
Monumental Architecture

p. 67,   "All the world's culture . . ." Peter Green, *The Parthenon* (New York: Newsweek, 1981), 155.

p. 67,   "The portion of the Parthenon . . ." Ibid, 147.

p. 69,   "Built mainly of large blocks . . ." Sacks, *Encyclopedia of the Ancient Greek World*, 63.

p. 70,   "a free-standing unit . . ." William R. Biers, *The Archaeology of Greece* (Ithaca, NY: Cornell University Press, 1996), 70.

pp. 71-72, "The Greek temple . . ." Edith Hamilton, *The Greek Way* (New York: Norton, 1993), 50-51.

p. 72, "There is the Doric column . . ." Thomas Craven, *The Pocket Book of Greek Art* (New York: Pocket Books, 1950), 44.

p. 74, "You should fix your eyes . . ." Thucydides, *The Peloponnesian War*, 149.

p. 74, " a special intimacy . . ." Martin, *Ancient Greece: From Prehistoric to Hellenistic Times*, 121.

p. 76, "Future ages will wonder . . ." Thucydides, *The Peloponnesian War*, 148.

CHAPTER SEVEN:
Athletic Games and Sport

p. 77, "In that quest . . ." David C. Young, *The Olympic Myth of Greek Amateur Athletics* (Chicago: Ares, 1984), 176.

p. 78, "All over Greece . . ." Hamilton, *The Greek Way*, 24-25.

p. 80, "The terms of the truce . . ." Judith Swaddling, *The Ancient Olympic Games* (Austin: University of Texas Press, 2008), 12.

p. 82, "Aren't you scorched there . . ." Ibid, 6.

CHAPTER EIGHT:
Enduring Military Traditions

p. 88, "Western armies [are] subject . . ." Victor Davis Hanson, *The Wars of the Ancient Greeks and Their Invention of Western Military Culture* (London: Cassell, 1999), 20, 22.

p. 89, "Hoplite warfare . . ." Ibid, 50.

p. 92, "Every shield protected . . ." John Warry, *Warfare in the Classical World* (Norman, OK: University of Oklahoma Press, 1995), 37.

p. 92, "left the property and culture . . ." Victor Davis Hanson, *The Western Way of War* (New York: University of California Press, 2009), 224.

p. 93, "So long as the phalanx . . ." Polybius, *Histories*, 509.

p. 93, "The two lines . . ." Xenophon, *Anabasis*, trans. W. H. D. Rouse (New York: New American Library, 1959), 38.

✿ Bibliography

Selected Books

Adkins, Lesley, and Roy A. Adkins. *Handbook to Life in Ancient Greece*. New York: Facts On File, 2005.

Arrian. *Anabasis Alexandri*, published as *The Campaigns of Alexander*. Translated by Aubrey de Sélincourt. New York: Penguin, 1976.

Biers, William R. *The Archaeology of Greece*. Ithaca: Cornell University Press, 1996.

Blundell, Sue. *Women in Ancient Greece*. Cambridge, MA: Harvard University Press, 2001.

Bowra, C. M. *Classical Greece*. New York: Time-Life, 1977.

———. *The Greek Experience*. New York: Barnes and Noble, 1996.

Cartledge, Paul. *The Spartans: The World of the Warrior-Heroes of Ancient Greece, from Utopia to Crisis and Collapse*. New York: Overlook, 2003.

Castleden, Rodney. *Minoans: Life in Bronze Age Crete*. New York: Routledge, 1993.

Connolly, Peter. *Greece and Rome at War*. London: Greenhill, 2006.

Davies, J. K. *Democracy and Classical Greece*. Cambridge, MA: Harvard University Press, 1993.

Flaceliere, Robert. *Daily Life in Greece at the Time of Pericles*. Translated by Peter Green. London: Phoenix, 2002.

Freeman, Charles. *The Greek Achievement: The Foundation of the Western World*. New York: Viking, 2003.

Grant, Michael. *The Classical Greeks*. New York: Scribner's, 2001.

———. *From Alexander to Cleopatra: The Hellenistic World*. New York: Charles Scribner's Sons, 2000.

———. *The Rise of the Greeks*. New York: Macmillan, 2005.

Green, Peter. *Alexander of Macedon, 356-323 BCE: A Historical Biography*. Berkeley: University of California Press, 1993.

———. *Alexander to Actium: The Historical Evolution of the Hellenistic Age*. Berkeley: University of California Press, 1994.

———. *The Greco-Persian Wars*. Berkeley: University of California Press, 1998.

Hanson, Victor Davis. *The Other Greeks: The Family Farm and the Agrarian Roots of Western Civilization*. New York: Simon and Schuster, 1999.

————. *The Wars of the Ancient Greeks and Their Invention of Western Military Culture*. London: Cassell, 2006.

————. *The Western Way of War*. New York: University of California Press, 2009.

Herodotus. *The Histories*. Translated by Aubrey de Sélincourt. New York: Penguin, 1996.

Hornblower, Simon, and Antony Spawforth, eds. *The Oxford Companion to Classical Civilization*. New York: Oxford University Press, 2004.

Kagan, Donald. *The Peloponnesian War*. New York: Viking, 2003.

Kebric, Robert B. *Greek People*. Boston: McGraw-Hill, 2005.

Knox, Bernard, *The Norton Book of Classical Literature*. New York: Norton, 1993.

Meier, Christian. *Athens: Portrait of A City in Its Golden Age*. Translated by Robert and Rita Kimber. New York: Henry Holt, 2000.

Martin, Thomas R. *Ancient Greece: From Prehistoric to Hellenistic Times*. New Haven: Yale University Press, 2000.

Pomeroy, Sarah B. *Goddesses, Whores, Wives, and Slaves: Women in Classical Antiquity*. New York: Shocken Books, 1995.

————. Stanley M. Burstein, Walter Donlan, Jennifer Tolbert Roberts. *Ancient   Greece: A Political, Social, and Cultural History*. New York: Oxford   University Press, 2007.

Shipley, Graham. *The Greek World After Alexander, 323-30 BCE*. London: Routledge, 2000.

Snodgrass, A. M. *Archaic Greece*. Berkeley: University of California Press, 1981.

Starr, Chester G. *The Ancient Greeks*. New York: Oxford University Press, 1981.

————. *A History of the Ancient World*. New York: Oxford University Press, 1991.

Thomas, Carol G., and Craig Conant. *Citadel to City-State: The Transformation of Greece, 1200-700 BCE*. Indianapolis: Indiana University Press, 2002.

Thucydides. *The Peloponnesian War*. Translated by Rex Warner. New York: Penguin, 2008.

Young, David C. *The Olympic Myth of Greek Amateur Athletics*. Chicago: Ares, 1984.

❦ Web sites

Alexander the Great
http://www.livius.org/aj-al/alexander/alexander00.html

Ancient Greek Theater
http://www.richeast.org/htwm/Greeks/theatre/Theatre.html

The Ancient Olympics
http://www.perseus.tufts.edu/Olympics/

Aristotle and His Writings
http://www-gap.dcs.st-and.ac.uk/~history/Biographies/Aristotle.html

Clothing of Ancient Greek Women
http://www.richeast.org/htwm/Greeks/costume/costume.html

Democracy in Ancient Greece
http://www.bbc.co.uk/history/ancient/greeks/greekdemocracy_01.shtml

The Greeks: Crucible of Civilization
http://www.pbs.org/empires/thegreeks

The *Iliad*
http://library.thinkquest.org/19300/data/homer.htm

The *Odyssey*
http://library.thinkquest.org/19300/data/homer.htm

Perseus Project (large collection of information about ancient Greece)
http://www.perseus.tufts.edu

Women in Ancient Greece
http://www.womenintheancientworld.com/greece.htm

❀ Glossary

acropolis: "The city's high place"; a hill, usually fortified, central to many Greek towns; the term in upper case (Acropolis) refers to the one in Athens.

agoge: The various customs and institutions supporting Sparta's rigid military training system.

agon: A contest or struggle, a term the Greeks often applied to sporting events.

archon: A public administrator.

Areopagus: At Athens, an early aristocratic council and law court named for a hill in the city.

aristoi: "Best men"; aristocrats.

assembly: In many ancient Greek city-states, a meeting of citizens to elect leaders and discuss and vote on state policies.

astai (singular *aste*): Citizens who lacked political rights, most often applied to women.

bard: At first, an ancient Greek poet who recited verses from memory; later, simply a poet.

basileus: In Greece's Dark and Archaic ages, a respected chieftain who ruled a town or region.

Boule: "Council"; the Athenian legislative body that formulated laws and state policy.

bronze: A metal alloy composed of copper and tin.

catharsis: The act of purging one's frustrations or other emotions by watching someone else's suffering, for instance a dramatic character.

cella: The main room of a Greek temple, usually housing a statue of the god to whom the temple was dedicated.

choregoi (singular *choregus*): Well-to-do backers of plays and other theatrical and cultural events.

chorus: In Greek plays, a group of performers who stood and spoke in unison and interacted with one or more lone characters.

colonnade: A row of columns.

cosmos: The universe.

cuirass: A breastplate or other chest protection worn by an ancient infantryman.

dithyramb: Ceremonial poetry honoring the fertility god Dionysus.

Doric order: A Greek architectural style featuring columns with a rounded cushion and a simple, rectangular slab at the top.

Ecclesia: The Athenian Assembly.

epic poetry: Long, formal poems usually dealing with major events and featuring larger-than-life characters.

greaves: Bronze shin-guards worn by Greek hoplites.

gymnasium: A public facility in which men exercised, played sports, read, and attended lectures.

hegemony: "Leadership"; usually meaning political dominance.

hippodrome: An outdoor racetrack for horse and chariot races.

hopla: "Heavy equipment," specifically the armor worn by Greek infantrymen.

hoplite: A heavily armored infantry soldier.

hoplon (or *aspis*): The shield carried by a hoplite.

hubris: Arrogance.

Ionic order: A Greek architectural style featuring columns with curved scrolls, or volutes, at the top.

isonomia: Equality under the law.

kalokagathia: "Mind-body ideal"; a combination of physical and intellectual (or moral) achievement sought by some ancient Greeks.

logographai: Ancient Greek speech writers, especially those who composed court speeches.

lyre: A small harp.

lyric poetry: Short, informal poems most often dealing with everyday experiences and personal emotions.

megaron: In Bronze Age Minoan and Mycenaean palaces, a large hall, usually with a central hearth.

metics: In ancient Athens, resident foreigners, either Greeks from other city-states or non-Greeks.

oikoumene: "Inhabited world"; the term describing the large cultural sphere of the Greek-ruled lands during the Hellenistic Age.

orchestra: In a Greek theater, the circular stone "dancing" area in which the actors performed.

order: An architectural style, usually identified by the main features of its columns.

ostracism: An Athenian democratic process in which the people voted to banish an unpopular leader.

ostrakon (plural *ostraka*): A shard of pottery on which a citizen wrote during the process of ostracism.

othismos: "The shoving"; a military maneuver in which hoplites in the rear ranks of a phalanx pushed at their comrades' backs.

Panathenaea: The principal religious festival in ancient Athens.

panhellenic: "All-Greek"; used to describe ideas or events common to many or all Greek states.

pankration: A rough-and-tumble athletic event that combined elements of wrestling, boxing, and street-fighting.

panoply: A hoplite's complete array of arms and armor.

pantheon: The group of gods worshiped by a people or nation.

patron deity: The god or goddess thought to watch over and grant special protection to a city-state.

pediment: The triangular space on the front and back ends of a Greek temple created by the downward slope of the roof.

periodos: "Circuit"; the collective name for Greece's four main athletic games.

phalanx: A Greek military formation consisting of multiple ranks, with hoplites standing, marching, or fighting side by side in each rank.

physis: The first-principle, or nature's underlying physical basis.

polis (plural **poleis**): In Greece, a city-state, or tiny nation built around a central town.

sanctuary: The combination of a Greek temple and its surrounding sacred grounds.

sarissa: A long battle pike wielded by a soldier in the Macedonian phalanx.

skene: "Scene building"; a structure facing the audience area in a Greek theater and used for prop storage and scenic backdrops.

strategos (plural *strategoi*): In ancient Athens, a military general elected annually by the Assembly.

treasury: A small building having many of the same outer features as a temple but used for storing valuables.

tyrant: In ancient Greece's Archaic Age, a man who assumed power in a non-constitutional manner.

❀ Index

✤ Picture Credits